THE REVOLUTION AGAINST EVOLUTION

by Douglas B. Sharp

D0862993

Illustrations by
Richard Geer and Dennis Preston

Unless otherwise indicated, all Scripture quotations are taken from the *Authorized King James Version* of the Bible.

First Printing 1986
Revised Edition 1993

ISBN-0-938020-28-5
Copyright © 1986 Douglas Bruce Sharp

About the cover:

Glacier National Park is an outstanding example where the rock strata are not in the order that the theory of evolution predicts. The upper layers are Precambrian strata, which according to evolutionary time scale, are supposed to be 700 million years older than the Cretaceous strata underneath. Yet, there is no evidence for overthrusting.

TABLE OF CONTENTS

ACKNOWLEDGEMENTS

The following people made it possible for this book and ministry surrounding it to take place:

Editing: Dr. John N. Moore, Pastor Dave Williams,
Dr. Del Mokma, Roscoe Root

Cover: Phil Bowden
Illustrations: Rich Geer, Dennis Preston

Special Support: Dr. Erich von Fange, Dr. Del Mokma,
Dr. Jerry Bergman, Robert Liske, Roscoe Root, Shirley June,
David Conklin, David Skjaerlund, Rich Geer, Kevin Rich,
Kerby Rials, Eric Armbrustmacher, Ruben Ramon,
Jim Gatton, David Page, Paul Geer, Larry Perry

INTRODUCTION

A Christian can experience great joy knowing God exists and His word is true by examining the evidence around him. If you compare everything that man builds to God's creation, you see an incredible difference. As you observe anything man makes under a microscope, the closer you examine it, the more flaws you find. In comparison, God's handiwork in nature is orderly, and that order increases in detail and beauty the closer you examine it.

Reasons For Studying Creation

There are three reasons why we should study God's creation:

1. **Worship**. Scientific discoveries verify God's existence. As we examine nature, we give glory to God in His creation.

2. **Evangelism**. Evolution is a stumbling block that prevents people from receiving Christ. If we can remove that stumbling block, people become more open to the message of salvation.

3. **Building up of the Saints.** The more we learn about God's creation, it adds to the support we have for our faith in Jesus Christ. The demonstration of the power of God through the Holy Spirit provides primary evidence. Scientific facts verifying the word of God adds

to that faith, and provides a balance between the mind and the spirit.

Many believers say "I don't really need to have scientific evidence in order for me to have faith in Jesus Christ." I would definitely agree with them. Our faith should not rest in the "wisdom" of men, but in the power of God.[1] If we use that as an excuse, though, what impact can we make when an unbeliever comes to us with questions about the Bible, and asks why it conflicts with scientific theories? We need to have a ready answer for those who challenge our faith, so that they also have the chance to believe.

The conflict between science and the Bible needs resolution. The Bible does not conflict with true science, it opposes a belief system that wrongly calls itself science. Scripture describes this philosophy as "science falsely so called.[2]" It deserves challenge and exposure because evolutionary theories not only conflict with the Bible, but with scientific laws as well.

Now, where does the conflict take place? Creationists do not challenge micro-evolution, which describes the science of genetics and changes of characteristics within species. The contention is with mega-evolution, which is the idea of evolution from molecules to man. Mega-evolution is offensive because it is an affront to God as creator, and defies scientific reason. When we challenge evolution in this book, we are contesting mega-evolution.

Christians have not taken the time and effort to investigate the claims made by science that are contrary to the Bible. This neglect has provided a subtle and effective tool in the hands of Satan to destroy the credibility of the Word of God. If we doubt Genesis, then we undermine the account of the fall of man in the garden of Eden and the need for salvation. Genesis is foundational to our faith. Can we select what we want to believe in the scriptures and throw out the stuff we don't like or can't understand? Of course we cannot. Yet, that's what many Christians do.

There is tremendous pressure placed on believers to accept evolution as the only acceptable scientific choice. In most classrooms, we see evolution taught exclusively with no chance at all for the other side of the story to be presented. Because of that, most Christians are ill-informed on the subject, or divided. Often, they simply avoid the subject entirely. Because Christians neglect studying basic science, we find believers teaching evolution. This is happening even in Christian schools because of the lack of qualified science instructors aware of the scientific evidence for creation.

We need to lay hold of the strongholds which Satan has taken from Christianity. Before 1850, Christians dominated the arts and sciences, but when theologians compromised with evolution instead of challenging it, Christians gave up these subjects to atheism and unbelief. If we examine the history of the discipline of science, we find that many early scientists were believers in special creation. Pasteur, Mendel, and Faraday are examples. We should examine the lives of these early scientists and their lives to recapture their spirit and curiosity about God's creation.

Evolution has never been more vulnerable as it is today. The theory is under attack not only from creationists, but even within the ranks of unbelievers. Darwin's theory remains held together only by gossamer threads of guesswork. The facts of science, when exposed, testify against it.

Some people say that "the existence of God cannot be proven." The Bible states:

"For since the creation of the world God's invisible qualities—his eternal power and divine nature—have been clearly seen, being understood from what has been made, so that men are without excuse."[3]

With that statement, God is saying that we have no excuse for unbelief, since He has revealed himself in His creation. God has provided all the evidence we need to believe and trust in

Him through all He has created. Through His creation, He declares to the world, "I have made my existence blatantly obvious! If you miss salvation, it is not because I did not provide enough evidence. In fact, you have no excuse for your unbelief."

We must assess the evidence we have, and decide what we need for "proof" that God exists. God is under no obligation to prove Himself. There is plenty of evidence available at our hands that demonstrates the creative power of God. The key is to give the credit where credit is due, and worship Him for it.

I fail to understand why people do not thirst after God and desire to know Him. The benefits of knowing our Creator are tremendous. What better purpose is there in life than learning and following God's plan? The scientific facts compel me to worship Him, and by experiment I test my faith by applying His Word to my life.

Evolutionists often accuse Creationists of being biased because of our Christian faith. We're biased only with the same bias we have toward steak and potatoes with hot apple pie a la mode. We have sampled it and found it to be good!

Many have discovered their Christian faith by examining their surroundings, coming to the conclusion that this world around them cannot be just an accident, but God created it. I discovered this when I tried to combine amino acids together to form proteins. The sheer amount of work involved to do this convinced me of that. Proteins just do not naturally form by themselves: it takes a creative process!

The evolutionist has a "religious" faith at stake in this issue. His bias comes from his not wanting to deal with a personal God. If God has a personal plan for everyone, that means that each person has to choose God's plan over his own plan.

Of course, man has always thought he has a better plan. Part of the original sin of Adam was choosing his way apart from God. This is the source of spiritual pride: that a man's works can somehow buy the favor of God. Instead, we must choose to understand God's plan the best we can and follow it. If we make our own plans, we never experience God's best. What a terrible waste that is. But, that's the futile investment many scientists make! Evolutionists get grants for studying dinosaurs and ape-men. They write papers and do years of research propping up their theories. So, they naturally don't want creationism taught in the schools. Choosing a creationist point of view is a humbling experience. It strips all pretense of self-achievement away, exposing man for what he really is in the sight of God.

The theory of evolution is a natural result of man's desire to be independent of God. If we assume that God is creator, we have to acknowledge His lordship. A world-view based upon evolution provides a means of side-stepping the issue of admitting that Jesus is Lord. I intend to provide enough evidence in this book to get people to face this issue and deal with it.

One irritating dilemma that results from undertaking a study of God's creation is that we'll never finish the project. It seems that if we answer one question, six more pop up in its place. But, we can be content to live with a world view with open questions: that's when faith has a chance to work. Thank God our salvation is not dependent upon how well we have God figured out.

It's not my goal to figure out God. My objective is to expose the basic assumptions, tactics, and deceit behind the one who would rob us of our faith in Him. I do not fault evolutionists for their unbelief. My contention is not with them, but with the deceiver who blinds them. I invite you to join me in spiritual warfare against the father of all lies, who is Satan. That is the true nature of the revolution against evolution.

Avoiding Sectarianism

It is unfortunate that some people involved in the Creation-Evolution issue make their particular theory a point of division. Though the argument for a young earth creation model is very strong, I do not believe there is enough evidence scripturally or scientifically to be dogmatic about it. Even if there was, our attitude should be that of reconciling our brothers to the truth, not cutting them off fellowship.

God is not going to check our records to see if we believe the young earth theory, gap theory, day-age theory, or big bang theory before He lets us into heaven. It is possible to be wrong in our world view, and yet be right with the Lord in our heart. The reverse is also true; we can be totally correct in our thinking and still have no relationship with God. Some church people tack on the belief in a certain version of a theory as a prerequisite before they will fellowship with you. What a mistake! The purpose of the church is to draw people to Christ, not exclude them. All people are at different levels of faith, and we must make allowances for that.

We must not lose sight of the real value of studying God's creation: to find truth, to encourage others and to receive encouragement. Creation science is a useful tool when it removes stumbling blocks to faith. But we never need to defend God, He can take care of Himself. We need not defend His word, the Bible: it speaks for itself. Instead we offer to people a model of origins that makes it easier for faith to increase.

Remember: God is tenderhearted toward the evolutionist, as He is toward any person who is apart from him or bound. A judgmental attitude causes far more damage than wrong thinking. Our job is to reveal facts about creation that will stir up faith in God and cause liberty. Our attitude must be as one beggar telling another where to find bread. For the evolutionist and those whose world view differs from ours, we must offer a win-win proposition: personal acceptance and an offer to explore the facts to find the truth.

Beware of a mixed menu as offered by the cults: Creationism and the Watchtower; Creationism and British Israelism; Creationism and Mormonism; and even Creationism and New Age. This is a devilish trap that gets people to reject the truth with the error, or accept the error with the truth. Even worse, though, is Creationism and a bad attitude or lifestyle. In that case, people err in the spirit, though the reasoning may be sound and the doctrine Biblical.

Avoiding Compromise

As we show love toward those who disagree with us, we must continue to be bold in exposing the truth about God's creation, avoiding compromise. When God makes a statement in the Bible, He says, "Thus saith the Lord," not "This may be my opinion, but. . ." Nevertheless, many people adopt a relativistic perspective of the world, with no foundation for their faith.

Belief in evolution destroys a person's reason for faith in the Bible and ultimately in Jesus Christ. When presented with the theories of evolution, a student faces three choices: accept the theory of evolution and reject the Bible and Christ, reject the theory of evolution and accept the Bible as truth, or accept the theory of evolution, taking a giant "leap of faith" and believe the Bible in his spirit, though he doesn't really believe it intellectually.

Many Christians find themselves floundering in the last state. They may be saved by grace in Jesus Christ, but they drift aimlessly like a boat without a rudder or anchor, never deciding what is truth because they doubt the foundation for truth, Genesis. They believe, yes, but when you ask them why, they cannot tell you. This Genesis foundation is important, because without it we're only expressing opinions. If that is the basis for our faith, what would make our opinion any different from anyone else? That is the source of the "do your own thing" philosophy. Everyone is expressing opinions, and not looking to the Word of God as an authority. In this book, I provide solid reasons why I believe the Biblical account of creation over the theory of evolution. I invite you to test them for yourself.

I. ORDER FROM DISORDER?

Why is it always easier to make a mess than it is to clean it up? Can you assemble a jigsaw puzzle simply by dumping it on the table? Can you unburn a piece of paper? Suppose you ate a breakfast of scrambled eggs. Then imagine trying to un-eat those eggs, unfry them, unscramble them, get them back into their shell. Next, try to get them back into the chicken. Why does that sound ridiculous?

These are examples of the effects of a scientific law called the second law of thermodynamics. If we leave something alone, the natural tendency is for it to go from a state of order to disorder. The only way to reverse this situation is by creative intervention. One result of this law is if you want to create something, you must expend energy to the point that the disorder you generate is more than the order you create. In the transfer of energy from one point to another, there is always some waste left over.

The universe is bound by the second law of thermodynamics. It is constantly running down. The sun and stars burns up energy at a furious rate. There is not one place in the universe where we see energy created and stored up without the further expense of disorder. Therefore, the second law of thermodynamics demands that some time in the past, the universe had to be created and put in order.

The theory of evolution is in direct violation of the second law of thermodynamics. Evolutionists ask you to believe that the world started in a state of disorder, with life coming about by accident, and gradually increased in complexity and order. They say over the course of millions of years, it produced the world we have today. This idea is in direct opposition to what we observe. The theory of evolution hides behind great expanses of time. "Given enough time, anything can happen," evolutionists reason. If you consider the second law of thermodynamics, you'll find that's not true. Time is an enemy to order: as time increases, disorder increases.

A biology textbook offers this reasoning: "It has been said that living systems are an exception to the Second Law of Thermodynamics because they represent a greater state of order and organization than that found elsewhere in the universe."[1] But, they maintain that a regular input of energy sustains this apparent reversal of the second law.

The answer to that argument is that unless there is an energy conversion mechanism, a machine channeling the energy into something useful, the addition of external energy will speed the process of disorder, and evolution cannot occur. The second law of thermodynamics demonstrates creation!

This fact can be easily tested. Take any combination of chemicals off the shelf and expose them to the sun or any other energy source. Lay them on the sidewalk or out in the street. One of two things will happen, either they will not change, or they will break down into simpler components. Now, an evolutionist would argue that there might be a possibility that a complex chemical like a protein might form by accident. If that were to happen, it would over the long term break back down into simpler components. To produce life by chance, millions of these types of unlikely events would have to happen in the same place simultaneously.

I could argue that it is possible for all the water molecules in a glass of water to leap out of the glass. That would happen if they all moved in the same direction at once, instead of moving randomly. But you couldn't ever expect it to happen. It is the same likelihood that chemicals could randomly combine to form life.

The scriptures teach about the second law of thermodynamics. I believe that this law came into effect at the fall of man in the garden of Eden, and the introduction of death (Genesis 3:14-19). Part of the curse was that man now had to labor against this law as he worked. Paul in the seventh chapter of Romans laments his battle against the law of sin and death, but God brings victory through the power of the Holy Spirit (Romans 7:6-25, 8:1-16).

Let us imagine what might happen if we repealed the second law of thermodynamics. What would we have? We would have everything we would need for eternal life! If we did not not have decay, waste, or imperfection, we are describing heaven and eternal life. If God is the source of life, separation from him brings death and decay. Reunion with Him brings eternal life and salvation. Just as He set up the laws of nature in His creation, He brought forth spiritual laws that bring us life if we follow them. Jump off a cliff and attempt to violate the law of gravity, and you will meet sudden destruction.

If we obey God's laws, it leads to life. If we violate them, it leads to destruction in some form. But, we have the assurance that Jesus has conquered death through His resurrection, and that He is Life and can recreate what was destroyed by sin. I look forward to His promise that someday the curse will be removed, and we will enjoy eternal life.

SCRIPTURE REFERENCES

Genesis 2:17
Genesis 3:17-19, 22-23
Romans 7:7-25
Romans 8:1-28
Revelation 21:1-7
Revelation 22:1-6

QUESTIONS FOR STUDY

1. Why is it easier to make a mess than it is to clean it up?
2. Do inanimate objects organize themselves?
3. What does long periods of time do to the theory of eveolution?
4. Does the existence of life appear to violate the second law of thermodynamics?
5. What is the life in us that keeps us from decay and death?
6. What was Paul struggling with in Romans, chapter 7?
7. What is the remedy for the problem caused by the second law of thermodynamics?

II. HISTORICAL GEOLOGY and "FAULT FINDING"

Evolutionists look to "historical geology" for proof that evolution took place. Historical geology is the study of the fossils and rock formations found in the earth, and from the positioning of these fossils and rock layers called "strata" we derive information regarding the estimate of the age of the earth, and the estimates of the ages of particular layers of rock.

Historical geology is a misnomer, since evolutionists presume the ages to be **pre**historic. Radiometric dating is a method used to estimate ages of rock, a process where we analyze igneous rocks to find out how much radioactive material and subsequent by-products are in them. Using that information, scientists draw a conclusion about the estimated age of the rock. It is important to note that **sedimentary rocks**, which are the fossil bearing rocks, **normally cannot be dated** by this method.

Those of us who want to study the creation/evolution issue need to understand the background behind all "dating" methods used in "historical geology" and the assumptions involved. One paramount assumption of the theory of evolution is the idea of great expanses of time. We have already discussed why this assumption works against the theory of evolution, because of the laws of thermodynamics. Evolutionists are stuck with this concept whereas creationists don't have this problem.

Let's look at several underlying assumptions of the theory of evolution and examine them in the light of what we find in the rocks and fossils. The following is a list of these assumptions:

1. Evolutionists expect "younger" rocks to be on top of "older" rocks. The strata order should verify the theory of evolution.

2. Fossils can be "dated" by where they are found in the strata.

3. Strata can be "dated" by their fossils.

4. Certain fossils can be used as "index fossils" indicating the estimated age of the rock strata. This means that index fossils from two different time periods found in the same rock strata would be a problem.

Rock strata are not always found in the order that evolutionists expect. We find gaps between time periods. Rock sequences exist with "older strata on top of "younger" strata. Since the geologic column is foundational to evolution, this is a significant revelation.

What would it do to the theory of evolution if we find rock formations and strata in the opposite order evolutionists expect? That condition exists in many places.

Usually evolutionists explain such phenomena with the "overthrust" concept. That's where we find older rock

The Conventional Geological Column

Millions of Years	ERAS	PERIODS	EPOCHS	NOTES
	Cenozoic	Quaternary	Recent	
1			Pleistocene	man
13		Tertiary	Pliocene	
25			Miocene	
36			Oligocene	
58			Eocene	
63			Paleocene	mammals
135	Mesozoic	Cretaceous		
181		Jurassic		reptiles
230		Triassic		
280	Paleozoic	Permian		
310		Pennsylvanian		
345		Mississippian		amphibians
405		Devonian		
425		Silurian		
500		Ordovician		
600		Cambrian		shellfish
4500	Precambrian			algae

pushed up over younger rock. When an actual overthrust occurs, however, it leaves plenty of evidence: gouge (ground rock and powder), breccia, slickensides, and striated stone. In the following documented cases, this evidence is absent.

The Lewis Overthrust

First identified by Willis in 1901, this area encompassing Glacier National Park is more than 300 miles long and 15-50 miles wide, with Precambrian strata resting on top of Cretaceous.[1] The

LEWIS OVERTHRUST	
EXPECTED	ACTUAL
Cretaceous	**Precambrain**
Jurassic	**Cretaceous**
Triassic	
Permian	
Pennsylvanian	
Mississippian	
Devonian	
Silurian	
Ordovician	
Cambrian	
Precambrain	

fossils are in the wrong order. Evolutionists date the Precambrian rock at a billion years; the Cretaceous at 150 million years. The contact line between the two different strata is like a knife edge, suggesting that instead of an over-thrust, the strata were water deposited in that order. This contact line can be clearly seen at Chief Mountain, with the older strata resting directly on top of the younger.[2]

Upside-Down Geology
THE LEWIS "OVERTHRUST"

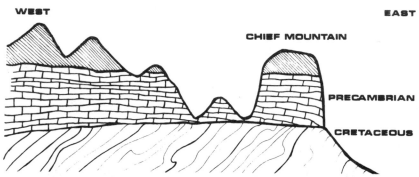

Since evolutionists suppose the Precambrian era to be the age before life evolved, and the Cretaceous period to be the age of the dinosaurs, the entire evolutionary time scale is at stake. The idea that such a large section of the Rocky Mountains uplifted and slid twelve to fifty miles to the east without leaving any evidence of movement is incredible. It is more reasonable to believe that the geological time scale is in error.

Evolutionists have proposed two theories, one that a massive fold got started in the earth's crust, sheared, and forced to the east,[3] the other that the block of strata slid down a slope.[4] The biggest problem with both theories is the size of the rock sheet. In order for an overthrust of the entire geologic column to occur, the original rock sheet would have been three miles high. A three mile high, 12,000 square mile rock sheet doesn't tend to slide anywhere or fold easily. The forces required to move it would have exceeded the crushing strength of the rock.

The Franklin Mountains

At a location known as West Crazy Cat Canyon near El Paso, Texas, scientists found massive Ordovician limestones on top of Cretaceous strata.[5] Evolutionists suppose the Ordovician period is the age of sea life, and Cretaceous is the age of the dinosaurs. Geologists found the fossils in the wrong order, and the strata are out of order, with no indication of movement between the two layers.

FRANKLIN MOUNTIANS	
EXPECTED	ACTUAL
Cretaceous	**Ordovician**
Jurassic	**Cretaceous**
Triassic	
Permian	
Pennsylvanian	
Mississippian	
Devonian	
Silurian	
Ordovician	

The Glarus Overthrust

At Glarus, near Schwanden, Switzerland, the order is Eocene (youngest) at the bottom, Jurassic (older) next, then Permian (much older) on top.[6] This would be an impossible order if the evolutionary geological time scale was true. We could explain two layers of strata out of order by overthrusting; three layers are unthinkable! The Matterhorn is another example of out of order strata found in the Alps.

GLARUS	
EXPECTED	ACTUAL
Eocene	**Permian**
Paleocene	**Jurassic**
Cretaceous	**Eocene**
Jurassic	
Triassic	
Permian	

The Empire Mountains

The Empire Mountains in Southern Arizona have a cap of Permian limestone resting upon Cretaceous rock. The contact line between the layers of rock is irregular, resembling the meshing of a gear.[7] If this was a real overthrust, the projections of the lower formations would have been planed off flat. There is no interbedding between the two rock sheets, nor is there any scraping, gouge or other evidence of movement.

EMPIRE MOUNTAIN DILEMMA

EXPECTED   **ACTUAL**

EMPIRE MOUNTAINS	
EXPECTED	ACTUAL
Cretaceous	**Permian**
Jurassic	**Cretaceous**
Triassic	
Permian	

HEART MOUNTAINS	
EXPECTED	ACTUAL
Tertiary	**Paleozoic**
Creaceous	**Jurassic**
Jurassic	**Tertiary**
Triassic	
Paleozoic	

The Heart Mountain Thrust

The Heart Mountains, just east of Yellowstone, are 50 different blocks of Paleozoic limestone scattered over a triangular area of 30 by 60 miles.[8] Underneath we find Jurassic and Tertiary sediments. Physical evidence for thrust faulting is absent, although a vertical fault may be possible.

The Great Smoky Mountains

Geological maps of the Great Smoky Mountains exhibit two large low angle thrusts, the Greenbriar thrust and the Great Smoky thrust, each containing out of order strata with little evidence of movement. According to a Geological Survey professional paper, "It is seen to be mostly a smooth clean-cut surface with little accompanying fault gouge or breccia, which dips at various but generally low angles."[9] The interpretation: although the fossils are out of sequence, there is very little evidence that the rocks have moved.

The Grand Canyon

The Grand Canyon presents a much different kind of problem for evolutionists. The Great Unconformity, a gap between two layers of strata where several geological "ages" are missing has interbedded layers of alternating Mississippian and Cambrian strata. How could two layers of rock really be separated by millions of years of earth history if they are shuffled like a deck of cards and intertongued?[10]

Scientists from the Creation Research Society have documented over 500 examples of strata mixups. John Woodmorappe, in an exhaustive article on the subject[11], outlines the world's

GRAND CANYON	
EXPECTED	ACTUAL
Mississippian	**Mississippian**
Devonian	Cambrian
Silurian	**Mississippian**
Ordovician	Cambrian
Cambrian	**Mississippian**
	Cambrian

stratigraphic makeup. He shows that very few places in the world reflect the stratigraphic order evolutionists expect. In another article, he also examines radiometric "dating" and its assumptions. He gives 438 examples where there is a 20% error or more between the date expected and the measured radiometric date.[12]

The Fossils Say No!

There are many documented cases where large fossils, such as trees or dinosaurs, extend through several layers of strata. These are called *polystrate fossils*, and are an indication that these strata were laid down in rapid succession. One such large formation exists in Nova Scotia.[13]

POLYSTRATE FOSSILS

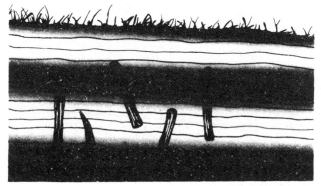

Extend Through Several Strata

Coal was formed about 300 million years ago, according to evolutionary dating. However, Erich von Fange[14] has documented several interesting human artifacts found in coal. These include:

1. a small steel cube
2. an iron pot

3. an iron instrument
4. a nail
5. a bell shaped metal vessel
6. a bell
7. a jawbone of a child
8. a human skull
9. two human molars
10. a fossilized human leg

Scientists have investigated several sites with human footprints in rock strata containing fossils from ages evolutionists believe are older than the emergence of man. One interesting and controversial example is the Paluxy River fossils near Glen Rose, Texas.

Here, dinosaur footprints exist alongside human footprints in the same strata. There are human tracks crossing dinosaur tracks, and dinosaur tracks that have blocked out human tracks in sequence. Investigators excavated some tracks out of the rock strata, and cross sectioned them. They showed a compressed layer pattern that indicated that they were genuine, not carvings.

Recent investigation at the Paluxy site has uncovered other unusual fossils such as a molar believed to be human, a cat print and a trilobite.[15] Such a mix of fossils from vastly different evolutionary "ages" found at one site in the same strata definitely raises questions about the validity of the assumptions underlying long ages.

Near Tuba City, Arizona, investigators found human footprints, handprints, and tracks of other mammals with the tracks of dinosaurs.[16] These tracks were well defined, with impressions of toes and fingers clearly visible. These tracks exist in the Chinle formation, which includes the Petrified Forest and Painted Desert.

Near Antelope Springs, Utah, sandal prints were discovered embedded in strata right on top of trilobite fossils (Cambrian).[17]

Other human footprints found in odd places:[18]

1. A fossilized leather sole of a shoe embedded in Triassic rock.

2. Human impressions were reported in a limestone slab in New Harmony, Indiana.

3. A rock outcrop near St. Louis, Missouri produced a large number of footprints. This was in crinodial limestone.

4. Footprints were reported in a quarry at Herculaneum, Mo.

5. Footprints unearthed in sandstone near Carson City, Nevada.

6. Footprints were discovered when a top layer of rock was removed from a sandstone formation near Berea, Kentucky.

7. A shoe print was discovered in a coal seam in Fisher Canyon, Pershing County, Nevada.

8. Footprints were found close to a lake near Managua, Nicaragua, underneath eleven strata of solid rock, 16 to 24 feet below the surface. Also found were traces of domesticated dogs and horses. Polished stone artifacts and projectile points were also found.

Fossilization Requires Quick Burial!

One major assumption of evolutionists is that long periods of time are required to form strata. But, in order for fossils to be preserved, they have to be buried quickly. When an animal dies and the carcass remains on the surface, it does not take very long for the process of decay to consume the remains completely, including the bones. The very fact that fossils occur as frequently as they do in the strata demonstrates a massive, quick burial. Sea shells remaining on the ocean floor quickly break up and disintegrate, unless they are buried. The existence of fossils is evidence for catastrophe!

That catastrophe, according to creationists, was the world wide Biblical flood of Noah that covered the earth. During the flood, ecological environments would have created successive layers, in the order of their relationship to the sea. Bottom dwelling shellfish would be buried first, then fish, then amphibians, reptiles, mammals and birds. Hydrodynamic sorting action of the water also would contribute to layering and separation. Coal formation, petrification, and fossilization all are processes that can occur quickly under the right conditions. The advantage of a flood model is that it explains out of order sequences in the fossils, whereas evolution does not have that luxury.

An illustration that burial is a requirement of fossilization is the fact that we do not find any buffalo fossil remains, though the buffalo was found widespread on this continent.

Radiometric Dating

What about radiometric dating? Doesn't that provide proof for evolution? To answer that challenging question, we need to examine the assumptions behind so-called "dating" methods to test their validity. Radiometric dating is a measurement of the ratio between a radioactive element and its by-products, estimating the age using the half-life of the radioactive element. The following are the assumptions of this method:[19]

1. The original composition of the rock was not contaminated with the by-product.

2. The half-life of the radioactive element remained constant, unaffected by catastrophic events.

3. No contamination of the by-products occurred after it solidified.

4. Leaching out or migration of the ions of the parent element did not occur.

5. Outside forces such as temperature, pressure, etc. remained constant and did not affect the dating of the rock.

If these assumptions are correct, then the radiometric dates are correct. But, there is no way for us to test these assumptions. If these assumptions are wrong, the method could yield erroneous dates far too old.

In the radiometric "dating" method, anomalies between expected dates and radiometric dates are common. Rather than to question the method and its underlying assumptions, scientists tend to accept the "dates" that support their conclusions and reject the ones that do not.

Suppose you have a burning candle sitting on the table. How long has that candle been burning? You can figure that out if you know the candle's burn rate and its original length. However, if you don't know the original length, or if you cannot verify that the burning rate has been constant, it is impossible to tell how long the candle was burning.

A similar problem occurs with radiometric dating of rocks. Since you cannot know the initial physical state of the rock, you can only guess according to certain assumptions based on what you know. These assumptions are based on the theory of evolution. Suppose conditions existed on the earth where there was a world wide flood? How would such conditions affect the radiometric dates?

Scientists have dated Hawaiian lava, samples from Mt. Vesuvius and other active volcanoes with the radiometric method. Since we know when these eruptions occurred, we can predict that if radiometric dating is valid, the dates given by the method would match the historic date. The dates yielded by the experiment were far too old, into the thousands and millions of years.[20]

To yield accurate dates, a timepiece must be accurate and sensitive. Imagine a strange hourglass with irregular shapes and sizes of sand in it. While the hourglass is running, you feed more sand into the top while sand leaks out the sides and bottom. Radiometric dating is like that. We don't know the original condition of the rock, we can't be guaranteed that the sample is uniform in consistency, and we don't know if any of the parent or daughter elements have contaminated or leached out of the sample. But, that is the method used to prove that the earth is billions of years old!

Why does the radiometric dating methods consistently yield old dates? One explanation is that the parent elements in the rock, potassium, rubidium, and uranium, are highly soluble in water in their ionized form, making them subject to leaching, especially in a flood environment. In contrast, the daughter elements, argon, strontium, and lead, are comparatively insoluble. Therefore, the ratio of parent to daughter elements would be low. Some creationists also believe that radiometric decay rates speeded up during the upheaval of the flood, yielding inaccurate dates.

Dinosaurs, Mammoths, Extinct Animals

Evolutionists seem to use dinosaurs as propaganda. Everywhere you look, there are dinosaurs in the textbooks, dinosaur toys, dinosaur cartoons, dinosaurs in the schools. Almost always next to the dinosaur there will be the phrase "millions and millions of years ago." No wonder whenever we see a dinosaur, we automatically think in terms of long ages! But, where is the proof that they truly lived so long ago? Like all the rest of the fossils, evolutionists date dinosaurs the same way, by the strata. In turn, the strata are Cretaceous because they find dinosaur fossils in them.

Can we explain dinosaurs satisfactorily with a creation model? Of course! Before the flood, conditions on the earth were much different. The Bible tells us that the age of the oldest person living before the flood was 969. Many people believe that the "firmament" mentioned in the creation account in Genesis[21] was a water vapor canopy surrounding the earth, shielding the earth from harmful radiation from the sun, providing a greenhouse effect and a warm climate.

One observation we can make is that reptiles, fish and other animals, do not stop growing as they age. The older reptiles get, the larger they get. Suppose a reptile lived for 900 years. What would you have? A dinosaur! Under such conditions, dinosaurs could have lived before the flood!

Those who hold to the vapor canopy model believe that the flood was caused by the collapse of this vapor canopy and the breakup of the fountains of the deep. The effect on this environment was such that it drastically reduced the ages of the people and animals who lived after the flood. Conceivably, dinosaurs (or their eggs) could have been taken aboard the ark, but not have survived long in the new environment. Examine the ages of the patriarchs before and after the flood in the Biblical account. You would observe a dramatic drop in the ages after the flood. This could have been due to the absence of the protective water vapor canopy that would have filtered out the harmful radiation from the sun.

The collapse of this water vapor canopy and the subsequent rain would have caused a drastic cooling effect upon the earth, and would have caused temperature variations and extremes. Explorers discovered entire carcasses of mammoths encased in ice in the Arctic, quick frozen and well preserved. The contents of the stomach of one such animal were analyzed and found to contain vegetation that suggests that the climate of the time was much milder than it is today.[22] They found bean pods still containing beans between the teeth.

What does the well preserved state of this mammoth and the condition of the carcass show us? The mammoth must have been frozen rapidly. The calculations from the study suggest that the mammoth was peacefully grazing on summer buttercups one lazy late July, then a sudden freeze of temperatures in excess of -150 degrees overcame him in a space of a half hour. What kind of cataclysm was this? Many believe that this was a cooling effect brought on the earth by the flood of Noah: an "ice age" that occurred after the flood.

Concerning the mammoth and the dinosaur, Job chapter 40 and 41 describes two animals, the behemoth and leviathan, animals whose descriptions strongly resemble dinosaurs.[23] Could these two animals have survived the flood to gradually become extinct? Since Job is the oldest book in the Bible, perhaps he was an eyewitness to these animals. Historical accounts abound of ancient legends of dragons, sea serpents and monsters. Is it possible that these stories have basis in actual encounters with dinosaurs? Drawings from these ancient writings bear an uncanny resemblance to reconstructions from dinosaur fossils.[24]

There is also fossil evidence for recent coexistence between man and mastodon. Rock carvings of the mastodon were found in Hava Supai Canyon in Arizona. A skeleton of a mastodon was found in Ecuador, evidently killed by Indians, with a circle of fires built around it for roasting of the flesh. Mastodon bones were found in a Mayan workshop in 1928, with smashed bowls and jars. They found a complete skeleton of a mastodon in an artificial salt pond constructed by Indians. This pond had a bottom of paved stones with the animal entombed by a sudden landslide.[25] Since the Mayan civilization peaked about 1000 AD, this would suggest a very recent date for the existence of the mastodon, well later than the predictions of evolutionists.

We who believe in the Biblical account of creation and the flood need not be intimidated by all the strange creatures found fossilized. The Bible tells us about a vastly different climate before the flood, which would account for mass extinctions of animals that would have thrived before the flood but not today. We note that the theory of evolution does not adequately explain all the problems associated with extinction of dinosaurs and woolly mammoths. Why was there a great dying out of these animals, unless there was a great cataclysm?

More evidence against evolution: some animals or fish presumed extinct for millions of years were found alive and well. The coelacanth, a supposedly extinct fish used for years as an index fossil, was caught and examined several years ago. Japanese fishermen reported dragging the carcass of a large dinosaur-like reptile resembling the supposedly extinct plesiosaur out of the ocean near New Zealand on August 27, 1977.[26]

Pleochroic Haloes

Microscopic radiation burns in crystal rocks called pleochroic haloes is evidence for an instantaneous origin of the earth, according to Robert Gentry, an expert in radiometric dating. Since they are imbedded in the rocks, the radioactive material must have been formed while the rocks cooled. When he discovered polonium haloes (half life of 138 days), he delivered a major blow to the idea of a gradual origin of the earth.[27] The question is, if the earth took "millions of years" to cool and then solidify, how was the polonium halo formed at all? If both cooled millions of years ago, why are uranium haloes found still radioactive? Short-life halos are a geophysical impossibility unless the Earth is far younger than the theory of evolution would have us believe. Dr. Gentry concludes that instant creation may be the only answer.[28]

To summarize, the following is a list of conclusions we can draw concerning "historical geology" as it relates to the creation/evolution question:

1. "Dating" of sedimentary rock cannot be accomplished by radiometric methods.

2. Evolutionists "date" strata by the fossils in them, and "date" fossils by their strata (circular reasoning)

3. In many places, "older" strata and "younger" strata are in reverse order.

4. "Unconformities" or gaps between evolutionary time periods are common in the rock strata.

5. There are many cases where fossils exist in rock strata not expected by evolutionists.

6. Mixed together in the same strata were fossils from different evolutionary time periods.

7. Polystrate fossils, or large fossils (trees, dinosaurs, fish), extend through several strata.

8. Human footprints and remains have been found in the "wrong" strata.

9. Fossilization requires quick burial. Otherwise, the bones quickly disintegrate under normal decay processes.

10. Radiometric "dating" depends heavily upon unproven assumptions of evolution.

11. Quick burial of dinosaurs and quick-frozen mammoths is evidence for a world-wide cataclysm.

12. Living "extinct" animals such as the coelacanth, supposedly dead for millions of years were used by evolutionists as index fossils.

13. Pleochroic halos are evidence for a young earth and an instant creation.

SCRIPTURE REFERENCES:

Job chapters 40-41   Psalm 104:5-9
Genesis chapters 5-9   II Peter 3:3-13

QUESTIONS FOR STUDY

1. List different "dating" methods evolutionists use for determining the age of rocks and fossils.

2. What are some assumptions of these "dating" methods?

3. What are some factors that might affect the date of a fossil or a rock?

4. List some examples of fossils found in the wrong order or in a wrong place.

5. What might the traditional evolutionary time scale correlate to according to the Biblical framework?

6. How do science textbooks or magazine articles popularize the theory of evolution and assume it?

7. What is the significance of the mammoth found frozen in the artic?

8. What are possible explanations for dinosaurs?

III. EARLY MAN

Over the last hundred years, evolutionists have gotten mileage out of fossil "cave men" or "ape-man" discoveries, using it as evidence that man is a product of evolution. As creationists, we must address this challenge, and provide answers that are satisfying. Consider these questions:

1. Are the fossils valid?

2. Are the methods used to estimate the age of the fossils valid?

3. Do the fossils follow a pattern, gradually increasing in complexity, resembling modern man as we reach the top strata, or are the findings scattered among the strata?

4. Are the interpretations of the fossil remains accurate, or is guesswork involved when evolutionists reconstruct them?

As we address each of these questions, we should examine each finding to know what these fossils mean.

If man evolved from the apes, what would we expect to find in the fossil evidence? The first thing we would look for would be a gradual increase in complexity in the fossils, until they looked like man. The "older" fossils would be found in the bottom layers, and the "more recent" fossils would be found in the top layers.

What would happen if we find fossils unmistakably human in the same strata or below the fossils considered to be ape-men? We could conclude that the ape-men could not have been ancestor to human beings, or that the ape-men were not ape-men at all. We have already discussed cases in the previous chapter where this is the case.

Piltdown man and the Nebraska man are two examples of how much speculation and presupposition plays a part in evolutionary thinking. Piltdown man was a hoax that fooled specialists for forty years: ape and human fossils doctored to look like they belonged together. The bones were treated with iron salts to make them look old, and the teeth filed to make them look like ape's teeth.[1]

Clarence Darrow used Nebraska Man as evidence in the Scopes trial, an ape-man built up from a single tooth that later turned out to be that of a pig. Another "skull" assigned to *Pithecanthropus* turned out to be an elephant's knee cap.[2]

Recently, an article in the *Science News* told of a researcher who identified a dolphin's rib as a collar bone of an ape-man. He claimed that the specimen resembled the clavicle of a pygmy chimpanzee and thought that the curve of the bone suggested that it walked on its hind legs.[3] The writer jested that the fossil should be called "Flipperpithecus!" An UPI press release revealed that a skull fragment hailed by experts as the oldest human fossil found in Europe, dubbed "Orce Man," was most likely a piece of the skull of a four-month old donkey![4]

Because of the fragmentary nature of the bones, scientists use much liberty of imagination when they reassemble them. Java man, discovered in 1891-1892, consisted of a left thigh bone fragment, part of a skull cap and three molar teeth. Eugene DuBois found these parts within a 50 foot range with other bones of animals. Recent finds have essentially identified him with modern man; the skull of a small woman, the femur completely human, and the teeth not belonging with the rest. He concealed the fact that he found other bones, totally human, in the same strata not far away.

Scientists have found over sixty specimens of Neanderthal Man. Evolutionists have for years used Neanderthal Man to prove their theory. But, some experts say that if you put a coat and tie on Neanderthal man, you couldn't tell him from anyone else walking down the street. Evidence shows that rickets and arthritis caused the bent over appearance of Neanderthal Man. Others suffered from an endocrine disorder such as acromegaly. This would explain their ape-like physical appearance.[5,6] Early scientists reasoned that Neanderthal was an ape-man because it just wasn't probable that all sixty specimens had rickets. Recently, a study proved the opposite; all sixty showed signs of rickets. Then, a Neanderthal was discovered buried in chain mail armor! That would put him in the time of the Middle Ages.[7]

A famous *Australopithecus* find is the Taung skull, named after the region in South Africa where it was discovered. Recently, specialists analyzed this specimen by computer aided tomography, to penetrate its rock-filled insides. These tomography pictures have convinced many theorists of human evolution to revise their earlier opinions that *A. Africanus* was more humanlike than apelike.[8]

One distinguishing characteristic of an ape is its U-shaped jaw, as opposed to a human V-shaped jaw. Many early finds of *Ramapithecus* classified as ape-men can now be classified as totally ape, based upon new evidence that their jaws are U-shaped.

Early human fossils are dated from their strata. This means that the dating of these fossils is dependent upon the assumptions of evolution. The problem is, truly human fossils were discovered in strata dated older than Australopithecines, supposedly the oldest ancestor to man. Where the radiometric date does not agree with evolutionary thinking, it is interesting how often they adjust and massage the data to fit the theory. The radiometric dating of "Lucy" is an example. After the original date of 3.6 million years became unpalatable, a geologist suggested that the date should be revised downward to 3 million years based upon comparative dating of similar volcanic tuff. Another date was 2.6 million years, then 2.9 million years, then 1.8 million years. Now, they believe that "Lucy" should be about two million years old.[9]

Researchers classified Lucy as an ape-man based upon a skeleton identical to a pygmy chimpanzee, except for a knee joint that was human in appearance. When a student asked Dr. Johanson where he found the knee joint in relationship to the skeleton, he at first refused to answer. Later he admitted that he found the knee joint a mile and a half away and 300 feet lower in the strata.[10]

The evidence points to catastrophic and rapid burial, with Lucy buried under volcanic tuff and *Zinjanthropus* buried in alternating and successive layers of shale and volcanic ash. These findings would fit the catastrophic Biblical explanation of the flood very well.

Fossilized skeletons of Cro-Magnon Man had a superior size and brain capacity to modern man. We could explain this with the Biblical idea that before the flood people lived longer and were healthier because God made the environment with the purpose for man to live forever.

Population statistics suggest that man has a recent origin. Using the present rate of growth, there would have been three billion people living before the flood. If every family had on the average of 4 children, who live an average of two generations, we would have the present world population in 1050 years. If it was 2.5 children, it would be 4300 years. If man was a half million years old, the present population would be roughly 10^{500} people. There isn't enough room in the universe to pack in all those people!

I don't think we need to go "ape" over fossil man. Conclusions about these fossils can only be speculative because of their nature, and cannot prove evolution. Every time a magazine announces that "scientists have found the missing link," check the following:

1. How complete are the fossils?
2. How were these fossils dated?
3. What other bones were found near by the fossils?
4. Can we explain these fossils with a Biblical model?

SCRIPTURE REFERENCES

Genesis 6:1-3   Genesis 5

QUESTIONS FOR STUDY

1. What is the "dating" mechanism used for estimating the age of fossil men?
2. Give a possible explanation why human fossils were discovered in strata "earlier" than so called ape-men fossils.
3. How are the fossils of ape-men assembled by scientists?
4. What would the population of the world have been at the time of the flood?
5. Give some examples where the evidence for ape-men was a deliberate hoax.
6. What motivation would someone have for searching for ape-men fossils?

IV. WHICH MODEL IS BEST?

I believe Christians need to have a world view, a model of origins, where they can reconcile science and scripture. Some people do not think they have the need to make this reconciliation. I agree that God does not give a "creation test" as a prerequisite for salvation. Being born again involves the spirit, primarily. But, to receive Christ, a person needs to be convinced that the Bible is true and is the word of God.

Anyone who studies science soon finds out that there is conflict between the theory of evolution and the Bible. Unless he is willing to live with this conflict, he has a definite need to have these questions resolved. Some people in this position don't bother to resolve the question, and compartmentalize their thinking, believing in God and in evolution. I feel that this is a dangerous position to take, since if we take it to its ultimate conclusion, it leads to the compromise and confusion of deciding which portions of Genesis are true.

Others put on spiritual blinders when it comes to the evolution question. They become masters at artfully dodging the study of science. To them, the question is simple: God created the universe and they believe it. I don't have much problem with that except that it is no help to those who struggle with the question. It is difficult to have answers if we avoid the question altogether. Evolution is not a side issue to those who stumble over it. If a parent avoids finding answers to the question of evolution, they risk losing their children to unbelief when they go to college and are confronted by this issue.

Regarding a model for the origin of the universe and the earth, there are only two possibilities: either God created it or everything happened by chance. If you reject the first model, you have no choice but to believe the second.

To believe the Biblical account of creation, we need to examine where scripture is very specific and certain. We also should point out where scripture does not contain clear information, and where we cannot establish certainty based upon scripture. It is important for us to know the word of God, what it specifically says, what it does not say, and to have the wisdom to discern the difference. It is not a wise idea to argue our pet theories, trying to establish them as doctrines without a solid foundation in God's Word.

I believe that if we use the law of "least scripture twisting" we will have the best chance of being correct. One way to know the correct translation is to give the Word of God to a child. Have him interpret what it says, not some professor who may be confused by too many opinions. I have to believe that God didn't write his Word with tricky language to confuse us. Instead, He made His Word plain and simple, so that all could understand and believe. If we are to be "full gospel" believers, Genesis should be taken at its plain natural reading.

Most Creationists will hold to the following ideas as certainties, well established from many different passages from scripture:[1]

1. God created all things, and continues to uphold and govern all things. God is absolutely sovereign and nothing is impossible with Him. God reveals to man

only what He chooses to reveal.

2. The Genesis account of origins is to be taken as literal history.

3. God created Adam and he descended from no creature.

4. Adam transgressed and the human race fell into sin, bringing vanity, misery, decay and death. Had Adam not sinned, there would have been no death for the human race.

5. Creation occurred in six distinct steps.

6. God appointed the heavenly bodies to be lights, signs, and to mark seasons, days and years.

7. God created during six sequential days and rested on the seventh.

8. The earth will perish and wear out like a garment, to be changed at the return of Christ.

9. God judged and destroyed mankind with a massive global flood.

Other points we cannot be as certain about because scripture does not discuss them. They may be briefly mentioned, or the meaning can be interpreted several different ways. The following points are logical conclusions based on the whole scripture. We can draw these conclusions based upon a natural reading of scripture and a utilization of the best principles of interpretation. Often, a scripture can be interpreted two different ways, and there can be two possible creationist teachings that result. Here is a list of these conclusions and their significance.

1. The time span mentioned in the Genesis account is days. Some hold to the idea that these were not 24 hour days, but were "ages" or long periods of time,

corresponding to uniformitarian ages as in the fossil record. My strong conviction is that the "day" does refer to the literal 24 hour period, since it is the most natural reading of the scripture. Also, after each "day" comes the description "and there was the evening and the morning." This is hard to reconcile with the day-age theory.

2. God did not mark the seasons, days, and years until the fourth day.

3. There is some uncertainty whether God created the sun, moon, stars and planets on the fourth day, or whether He simply appointed them to govern the day and night, and they existed as part of a vast eternal past. This "appointing" could have happened simply by removing a cloud cover. If "heaven" means "firmament" or atmosphere, this explanation is a possibility. The alternative is to challenge the distances of stars estimated by astronomers, and question theories of physics, relativity and the speed of light. Some creationists make a good case for this, providing strong evidence that God created the universe the same time He created the earth.

4. It is certain from scripture that the earth will wear out like a garment and perish. It is probable we can carry out the same assumption for the universe, that it also will wear out and perish, to be changed to give way to the new creation in Christ.

5. If we read the Bible in its most natural language, it is difficult to imagine gaps taking place in the creation narrative which would allow for an evolutionary scale of time. Many believe there was a gap between Genesis 1:1 and 1:2, where God destroyed a kingdom on the earth set up by Satan, allowing for millions of years of fossil accumulation. Others believe that there are gaps in the genealogies. Theolo-

gians proposed the Gap Theory as a compromise between evolution and the Bible. But, assuming a gap is an argument from silence. It seems unlikely that God would fail to mention millions of years of earth history in His word if it really happened. The biggest problem with the gap theory is that it assumes a great extinction and dying out of an evolutionary pre-world long before death came into the world at the fall of man. Believers in a recent creation place the date of creation between 6,000 and 10,000 years ago.

6. God exercises his supernatural power in the earth through altering of natural processes, which would affect what scientists observe. The flood of Noah is the primary example.

7. The flood of Noah accounts for most of the sedimentary geology we find in the strata, and the fossils found in the strata represent antediluvian creatures buried in the sequence corresponding to their environment. Other pre-flood and post-flood catastrophes could account for other burials of creatures and geological landforms.

8. The antediluvian world was a tropical environment, allowing people (and animals) to live more than 900 years.

9. Biblical "kinds" (after their kind) probably do not correspond to evolutionary species.

Theistic Evolution

There are three major creationist viewpoints, the Day-Age Theory, the Gap Theory, and the Flood Geology or Recent Creation model. I do not consider theistic evolution to be a creationist framework, since it is not an attempt to reconcile scripture, but is simply saying "evolution occurred, but God helped it along."

Theistic evolution is an embarrassment to Christianity, a "cop out." The theistic evolutionist believes that Genesis is only an allegory about how things came about, not how it really happened. I saw a Sunday School lesson once that said that Genesis was a myth, but it was a "true myth." What a dilemma these pathetic theologians find themselves in, wanting to believe, but cannot.

Those who take that stand ultimately end up questioning the authority of scripture. If Genesis cannot be taken as truth, which parts of scripture do we select to believe and which don't we believe? Would God allow His word to be confused by human ideas, or would He give us false information? God did not write Genesis in an allegorical style. It is matter-of-fact, as if it were a news report. It is a mistake to try to read into scripture interpretations that are beyond its plain, natural reading.

Theistic evolutionists place more faith on human reasoning than on Biblical revelation, without considering the scientific or theological implications. Consider the origin of the theory of evolution. Were the original promoters of evolution men of faith in God? How can we reconcile a humanistic philosophy to the Bible when evolution is by design an atheistic philosophy?

When you study any philosophy or religion to see if it is the truth, examine its roots and its fruits. What kind of people originated it? What kind of people are involved in it today? What difference does it make in their lives? Another hint is to examine the spirit behind it. For example, there is an occult atmosphere surrounding UFO's that generates a deep spirit of fear. This spirit is definitely not of God. An argumentative and intimidating spirit is another telltale sign of error.

The Day-Age Theory

This theory resembles theistic evolution, but proponents attempt to reconcile scripture with the theory of evolution by claiming that the Biblical word "day" really means millions of years, and "created" really means "evolved," and so forth. This framework involves the least amount of challenge to the theory of evolution. It says that God gave the initial creative impulse to each era, and supervised the gradual development of each species.

The Day-Age theory does not fit a plain and natural reading of the first chapter of Genesis. Nevertheless, many people seem satisfied with this explanation, and attempt to retain a literal view of scripture elsewhere. I believe that we do not need this compromise with evolution. I think it is dangerous and that better models are available. The phrase, "and the evening and the morning" follows the description of each day's creation activity. Such a phrase would hardly fit a description of long periods of millions of years.

The Gap Theory

The Schofield Bible and Dake's Commentary are examples of works in contemporary use that promote the Gap Theory. Also known as the ruin-reconstruction theory, the Gap theory proposes that the original creation took place millions of years ago, and there was a "gap" between Genesis 1:1 and Genesis 1:2 where a cataclysmic destruction took place connected with the fall of Satan and the dark angels. The reasoning here was that the world in Genesis 1:2 "became without form and void, and darkness was upon the face of the deep." The words for "without form" (tohu) and "void" (bohu) mean desolation, confusion and an indistinguishable ruin. From this point on, according to this theory, God began a new creation work, which took place over six literal days.

The Gap Theory places the dinosaurs and millions of years of evolution in this gap, leaving mammals and men as part of the new creation. Gap theorists give Isaiah 14:12 as proof that the fall of Satan took place in this gap.

Similar problems crop up with the gap theory as they do with the Day-Age theory. It is a compromise with evolution that is unnecessary. Unlike the day-age model, the gap theory is catastrophic, and in that sense it is a lot more like the recent creation model that will be discussed next. But, gap theorists are unwilling to challenge evolutionists on the issue of time and long ages. We need to ask the question: would we come to this conclusion based upon a natural reading of scripture if we did not have evolutionary bias? Did this interpretation of scripture exist before Darwinism?

Certainly, theologians can come up with clever ways to make scripture sound like it fits the idea of long ages. Redefine the meaning of a word here, make another assumption there, and a compromise that will satisfy some people can be made. But, the basic problem with the theory of evolution is not reconciling it with theology, because the scientific evidence is against it.

Problems with the Day-Age and Gap Theories

Although I'd prefer that someone believe in either the Day-Age or Gap theory than be an atheistic evolutionist, there are enough problems with both models from both a scientific and theological perspective to generate erroneous teaching.

Exodus 20:11 tells us that "in six days the Lord made the heaven and the earth." That statement alone confounds the idea of long ages or gaps. This verse is used in the same context as the six days of the week, referring to the Sabbath day in the ten commandments. The scripture wouldn't talk about a literal day of the week in one sentence, then tie it with six "indefinite periods of time" in the next. Instead, Exodus 20:8-11 ties together the seventh day of the Sabbath to the seventh day of creation. The statement after each creation day about "an evening and a morning" gives definite confirmation that the scriptures are talking about a literal 24 hour day, not an indefinite period of time.

Exodus 20:11 also ties the creation of the heaven with the creation of the earth in the six days, ruling out the possibility of a gap. If the writer of Genesis wanted to convey a long period of time for the creation, he could have used the Hebrew word "olam" instead of the word "yom." Exodus 31:15-17 repeats this assertion.

The Day-Age and Gap theories utterly fail in their attempt to reconcile scripture with the theory of evolution. The order of creation in Genesis doesn't fit the imagined evolutionary scheme at all, in fact the first creatures mentioned specifically in the creation account were birds and whales! There are not six distinct evolutionary ages corresponding to six "creation periods" in the Bible.

The Gap theory crams the entire evolutionary history of decay, death and struggle between the first two verses of the Bible, but death never occurred until after the fall of man. There is no indication that the fall of Satan from heaven produced a cataclysm here on earth. God cast Satan to the earth only after his rebellion and fall. This is the overriding objection to these theories; if we take them to their ultimate conclusion, they make God out to be the author of evil and confusion![2]

Since God created the world and called it good, Satan could not have rebelled and occupied the garden until some time after creation. Gap theorists use Ezekiel 28 to prove their theory, but ignore verse 13-17 where Satan (who was the spirit behind the King of Tyre in the prophecy) was in Eden when his heart was turned against God to be subsequently cast out of God's presence. Therefore, his fall could not have occurred before the six day creation of Eden.

One idea proposed by a Gap theorist was that there must have been two Edens, one of mineral beauty ruled by

Satan for millions of years, and the other created or re-stored by God![3] But comparing Ezekiel 28:13 with Genesis 2:12 shows that the Eden of Genesis was one of mineral beauty also. We need not strain the scriptures to include an evolutionary explanation.

Unfortunately, most theologians find that challenging evolution is too big of a task for them to take on. Overwhelmed by complex arguments and buried in scientific jargon, they are intimidated and forced into compromise.

Once we understand the magnitude of the error of evolution and how much it lacks observational support, we realize the foolishness of trying to compromise with it.

The Recent Creation Model

The recent creation model directly challenges evolution from a scientific point of view, and examines the assumptions involved in the scientific methods used in establishing "dates" of rocks and fossils. According to this model the earth is young, and there are no gaps in the Biblical record. The flood is an explanation for the strata sequence.

Scientists and Christian scholars who believe this model have assembled much information challenging the idea of a four billion year old earth. Because of this evidence, we do not have to fit long ages into a creation model. These scientists have developed a theoretical model of the earth which describe the conditions that existed prior to the flood and creation.

According to this framework, the earth at the time of the flood was vastly different from today. A "firmament" or atmospheric canopy made up of water vapor provided a favorable environment caused by the greenhouse effect. Plants and animals grew to very large sizes, and had life spans that exceeded 900 years. This canopy filtered out the radiation that now penetrates to the earth from outer space.

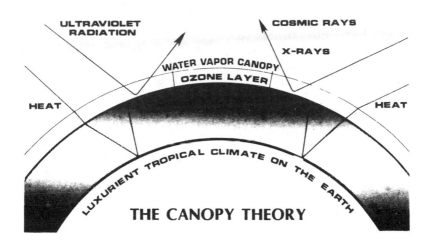

THE CANOPY THEORY

It was in three layers, an outer ozone layer thicker than it is today, a central water vapor layer trapping long wave earth rays, and an inner atmosphere with a higher concentration of carbon dioxide and water vapor. This inner atmosphere covered the earth like a warm blanket, and watered the earth with dew.[4]

The Biblical Flood could have been the result of a combination of the fall of the water vapor canopy and bursting forth of subterranean springs in the ocean. Some believe that ice particles from outer space were directed onto the poles by the earth's magnetic field. This may have triggered the fall of the water vapor canopy. Others believe volcanic activity could have condensed the canopy as a result of the breaking up of the fountains of the deep.

Either model would have caused an instantaneous blizzard at the poles, with temperatures plummeting to -150° F, quick freezing all life there. This would help to explain the quick-frozen mammoths found in the Arctic, and ice sheets in Antarctica that go as much as 5,000 feet below sea level.

Others believe an "ice age" was a result of the cooling effect of the wind God sent after the flood causing the waters to recede, or a result of centrifugal force bulging the earth with the flood waters at the equator, leaving vast ice masses at the poles.

During the flood, the creatures with the highest density would be buried first such as shellfish, followed by sea creatures, amphibians, reptiles, then land animals, which would escape to higher ground before burial took place. The moving water also provides a mechanism for sorting and selecting deposits. The settling velocity of large particles is directly related to their size, density, and spherical shape. With tides of 5,000 to 10,000 feet, there would be much displacement of soil. Tremendous pressures were placed upon all the buried matter, petrifying wood and fossilizing everything in a matter of hours. The sedimentary sequence represents this order: successive layers laid down in massive tidal depositions of sediment.

Every continent is covered with thick layers of strata, which shows that the flooding took place on a massive, global scale. Strata are not being formed today, except at a very small scale at the mouth of rivers.

A proposal explaining the continental "plates" is that with the breaking up of the fountains of the deep came the separation of the continents. This provided an ocean floor for the water to drain into after the flood. Some believe that earth expansion accompanied continental drift.[5] The earth's crust rides upon a layer of molten rock underneath it. The pressure of additional weight of water would have caused the earth's crust to split and spread apart. This would explain why there are far more spreading zones in the earth's crust than compression zones. The ocean floor around Antarctica is evidence for this: spreading zones surrounding the entire Antarctic plate.

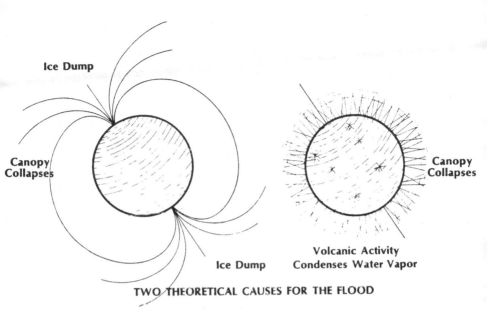

Ice Dump

Canopy
Collapses

Canopy
Collapses

Ice Dump

Volcanic Activity
Condenses Water Vapor

TWO THEORETICAL CAUSES FOR THE FLOOD

Much research in creation science is continuing under the recent creation framework. Though there are many versions of this model and plenty of room for speculation, a young earth explanation is most satisfying from both a scientific and scriptural point of view.

Young Earth, Ancient Cosmos

Some creationists believe that God created the earth, the solar system and visible stars during the creation week in Genesis, but believe the rest of the universe existed before the creation. This scenario dismisses the problem of an old universe based upon the apparent vast distance of stars without having to challenge contemporary physical light theories.

This model is based upon the definition of the word "heaven" found in Genesis 1:1 and Exodus 20:11. In Genesis 1:8, God called the created firmament heaven. It is likely that the firmament refers to the atmospheric canopy that offered protection to the pre-flood world. If that is the case, God could have created the cosmos much earlier, not necessarily during the seven day creation week.

An argument against this viewpoint is the statement "and He made the stars also" found in the account of the fourth day.[6] A counter argument would be that God created the stars visible from the earth on that day, or that He simply revealed them by removing a cloud cover.

Since God is eternal, the possibility exists that the universe also may be eternal, unless of course God created time itself at the beginning and God resides out of our time-space realm. But much of physical light theory taught today is based upon evolutionary assumptions. Several creationist physicists have proposed light theory models based upon different assumptions that would allow for a young universe. These models are discussed in the chapter on stars and planets.

The summary of the creation work found in Genesis 2:1 and 2:4 poses a problem for the idea of an ancient cosmos.

"Thus the heavens and the earth were finished, and all the host of them." (verse 1).

"These are the generations of the heavens and of the earth when they were created, in the day that the Lord God made the earth and the heavens." (verse 4).

Both verses refer to the heavens in the plural, and verse 1 refers to "all the host of them." If the writer was trying to convey that God finished all the heavens during the creation week, this would be a good description. There still may be an outside chance that part of the distant cosmos visible to us through our telescopes may be outside the realm of space and time, part of the eternal past. This is an argument from a scripture vacuum, and it would have to be beyond the "heavens" described in these verses.

A young earth-ancient cosmos model would present fewer major theological implications than the Day-Age or Gap theories which conclude that there was a long period of death and struggle before Adam. Those who want to remain scriptural, but don't buy the idea of a young universe may find some refuge with this model.

Many other models have been proposed for the origin of the earth as it relates to Genesis. That is the challenge of the creation scientist: to take the evidence and formulate the best picture of what happened in the past.

Advantages of Creation Viewpoints

1. God could have created the earth in any time frame he chose to. Evolutionists, stuck with long ages, have to contend with the laws of thermodynamics, and the fact that time is an enemy to evolution.

2. Creation provides a simple explanation for the origin of life.

3. The Biblical flood explains the geological puzzles found in the fossils.

4. The apparent young age of man is directly explained by the Biblical record.

5. The creation model is more consistent with the laws of thermodynamics, and explains the universal degradation we can see in the universe. Evolution is directly contrary to these laws.

6. Creation is more satisfying from a philosophical point of view. If one assumes an evolutionary viewpoint, he must conclude that he is a product of blind chance and life is meaningless. Man's existence is meaningless under such a world view.

SCRIPTURE REFERENCES

Genesis 1	Romans 5:12
Exodus 20:8-11	I Corinthians 5:21
Exodus 31:17-18	Genesis 3:17
Genesis 1:31	Romans 8:20-22

QUESTIONS FOR STUDY

1. Give a critique of each Creationist viewpoint, and decide how much they agree with scripture.

2. What problem does Exodus 20:8-11 and Exodus 31:17-18 cause for the Day-Age Theory?

3. Can we reconcile the idea of millions of years to the Bible? Why?

4. What evidence is there in the fossils of a flood and a recent creation?

5. If a person lacked knowledge of the theory of evolution or uniformitarianism, would he propose the Gap Theory from a strict reading of scripture? Why?

V. ANIMALS THAT PROVE CREATION

A fundamental concept of the theory of evolution is that of gradual change from a "primitive," less complex organism into a highly structured organism over an imagined period of millions of years. How valid is this idea? Can we really verify the evidence supporting this idea? There are many animals existing today that totally defies evolution by their very existence. This chapter will give examples of some of these animals and explain the problems they give the theory of evolution.

The logical frame of reference used in concluding that these animals could not have been the product of evolution is called an indirect proof. The way this works is to assume the opposite of what you wish to prove, proceed logically until you reach a contradiction or an impasse, then conclude that the alternative is true. In this chapter, we will use the concept of indirect proof with evolution, proceed logically until we reach an dead end, leaving creation as the only other alternative.

The realization that each animal is an interdependent, interrelated system was the greatest factor that influenced me to believe that evolution could not have occurred. To survive in a particular environment, an animal has to have features that work in that environment. For example, air breathing animals needs lungs. Flying creatures need wings. If evolution is valid, transitions from one environment to another had to have occurred. If such transitions are impossible, evolution is impossible!

Gradual evolutionary change from one species to another requires many mutations and genetic changes. But, the fossil record exhibits anything but gradual change. There is a gap between living systems and non-life, invertebrates and vertebrates, fish and amphibians, amphibians and reptiles, reptiles and birds, reptiles and mammals, and mammals and man.

Dolphins and Whales

We can demonstrate one such transition problem by using the example of dolphins and whales. These mammals bear their young alive and breathe air, yet spend their entire lifetime in the sea. Presumably, in order for dolphins and whales to have evolved, they must have originated from a land mammal that returned to the water and changed into a sea creature. But dolphins and whales have so many remarkable features upon which their survival depends that they couldn't have evolved! It would be a lot like trying to change a bus into a submarine one part at a time, all the while it is traveling at 60 miles per hour.

The following is a list of transitions evolutionists have

to account for in the dolphin in its evolution from some unknown land dwelling pre-dolphin:

- The nose would have to move to the back of the head.
- Feet, claws, or tail would be exchanged for fins and flippers.
- It would have to develop a torpedo shaped body for efficient swimming in the water.
- It would have to develop a system to prevent the "bends" from occurring upon rapid ascension from a dive.
- It would have to drink sea water and desalinize it.
- It's entire bone structure and metabolism would have to be rearranged.
- It would need to develop a sophisticated sonar system to search for food.

Could the dolphin acquire these features gradually one at a time over a period of millions of years? What about the transitional stages? Would they have survived with just some of these features? Why is there a total absence of transitional forms fossilized?

Consider the whale and its enormous size in comparison with the plankton it feeds upon. The whale is a nautical vacuum cleaner, with a baleen filter. While it was "developing" this feature, what did it feed upon before? For me, it takes a great stretch of the imagination to picture the evolution of dolphins and whales.

The Duckbill Platypus

The explorer who first saw a hide of the duckbill platypus thought that it was composed of the hides of several different animals sewn together as a joke. Later, when a

The Duckbill Platypus

preserved specimen was brought to him for dissection, he finally declared it outrageous, but genuine!

The more you study the duckbill platypus, the more problems you find for evolutionists. Here is a list of some of its features:[1]

- It is a fur-bearing mammal.

- It lays eggs, yet suckles its young.

- It has a duck-like bill, which has built within it a heat sensitive worm finding radar.

- Its tail is flat like a beaver's, yet furry.

- It has webbed feet in front, clawed feet in the rear.

- The reproductive systems are uniquely different from the rest of the animal world, but mostly mammalian in nature.

- The only other known egg-laying mammal, the echidna or spiny anteater, is much different from the platypus.

Can you imagine what a pre-platypus might have looked like? Nothing in the fossil record gives us a clue about the origin of this animal, which is an outrage to evolutionists. This animal does very well in its natural environment in spite of its unusual features. To look at it, it would appear that this animal was pieced together from a variety of completely different animals.

The Koala Bear

Koala bears[2] are marsupials that spend nearly their entire lives high in eucalyptus trees. Their diet consists of eucalyptus leaves toxic to humans. They survive without drinking water or shelter, survive high temperatures by panting, and a well insulated coat protects them from the cold.

One of the greatest "advances" of man according to the theory of evolution is the grasping hand with the opposable thumb. But, many apes also have a foot with an opposable great toe. Not to be outdone, the koala not only has an opposable great toe, but two opposable digits on each hand.

Now, also, the first digit of the foot lacks claws, but the second has two claws! Consider the evolutionist's argument for a claw to migrate from one toe to another over eons of time!

What about the unique pouch that opens aft? This feature is similar to that of the wombat, which is a completely different animal than the koala. What could the ancestry of the koala have been to account for these features, especially since transitional forms are missing in the fossils?

Most marsupials are confined to the isolated continent of Australia. Why then is the opossum so widespread in America? It is highly unlikely that one species of marsupial would be so highly removed from its ancestors.

This Theory Is For The Birds!

Proponents of the theory of evolution would have us believe that reptiles began to grow appendages on their back as extensions of scales, and these appendages supposedly developed over periods of millions of years into wings and feathers. Then, they believe that these reptiles began to climb trees and attempted to jump out and fly. Imagine all the ancestral birds attempting to do this until one day one of them had wings structured properly and took off and flew.

There is nothing that is gradual about a transition from a land environment to an air environment, or a land to sea, or sea to land. Such a transition does not take millions of years, either you can fly or you can't; either you breathe air or have gills.

One of the most complex structures in the animal kingdom is the feather. The feather is lightweight, yet very strong and sturdy. It is made up of a network of fibrils that interconnect with one another in such a way providing the best economy of surface area for the weight. There is a main stem serving as the main support for the feather. It branches out into tributary stems, each of which branches again until they interconnect by using hooks and barbicels.

How would a reptile react to feathers on his back? He'd probably pull them out! Such structures in a transitional form would be detrimental to a reptile.

Some birds have unique structures that enable them to perform specialized functions in nature.[3,4] The woodpecker is such an example. He has special shock absorbers in his beak and skull providing protection from the severe migraine headaches that might otherwise result from his hazardous occupation.

Imagine all the poor prewoodpeckers knocking themselves out, getting their beaks stuck in trees until this feature "evolved." Most birds have three toes in front and one behind. The woodpecker has two in front and two behind to enable him to grasp onto the side of a tree and peck away. He also has stiff tail feathers to support him and a long sticky tongue designed for fishing the insects he feeds on out of the holes he pecks in the trees. We have to conclude, God designed him for his special occupation.

Consider the water ouzel, a bird that not only flies in the air, but swims underwater with his wings![5] He also strolls on the bottom of the stream, overturning rocks with his beak and toes to feed on various water creatures. Air sacs provide buoyancy, enabling him to rise to the surface. He "blows his tanks" to submerge. Since he does not have webbed feet, he uses his wings as underwater oars.

He normally makes his nest behind a waterfall, through which he must pass to reach his front door. He makes his nest out of living moss, which is kept alive from the spray of the cascade.

How many eons of diving school did this bird endure before he mastered the delicate balance of the air and water environments? These functions would have to be perfected before our skinny-dipping friend would ever discover the juicy morsels on the bottom of the stream.

Bird migration poses a problem for evolutionists. How does one account for birds like the Arctic tern that migrates from pole to pole, and returns to the same nesting spot each year? How does one account for this apparent design if we rule out creation by God? The Phalarope is a bird who doesn't follow the normal pattern where the male gathers the food and the female sits on the eggs. Instead, it is the male who has to assume all the housewifely chores of nest building, incubation, and family feeding. Only one of two options is available: either juggling of the genders existed from the beginning or "Mother Nature" had to experiment with some bizarre transitional match making.[6]

Consider, though, the broader picture. What was the origin of sex and the roles each sex plays? Courtship behavior, sex roles and reproductive activity vary almost from species to species. This is an indicator of special creation. When did the two sexes diverge? According to evolution, a long slow process over millions of years created the sexes. But, reproduction is either asexual or sexual, there is no in-between. Even if some mutation created a male sexual creature, it would not reproduce unless the same mutation occurred in matching female as well!

Hmmmmmmmmm!

The smallest bird in nature, and one of the most amazing is the hummingbird.[7] Weighing only 1/14 of an ounce, he has much in common with a helicopter, flying backward and sideways and hovering in midair. Its rate of metabolism is so high that it must feed almost constantly. But,

since there are no rods in the hummingbird's retina for night vision, its vital processes shut down to a state of hibernation at night. The nest of the hummingbird is not much bigger than a postage stamp, made out of thistledown and cobwebs. But, built into this pint-sized bird is one of the most complex flight mechanisms known. Consider the following:

- The quill of the feathers is considered stronger for its weight than any structure designed by man.

- Flexibility of the quill allows the primary feathers at the wing tip to bend upward with each downbeat of the wing. This produces the equivalent of pitch in a helicopter.

- The quill constantly changes shape to meet the requirements of air pressure and wing position.

- The leading vane of the feather is narrower than the trailing vane. This feature causes the wing to operate like a propeller to give both lift and propulsion.

- The wing is an efficient double-jointed foresail, the inner half sloping at a slight angle to give lift like the wing of an airplane, while the outer half acts like a propeller.

- There is a jet assisted takeoff mechanism. A tuft of feathers at the junction of the wing adds extra airfoil surface during landing and takeoff.

- Enlarged muscles to operate the wings; almost 3/4 the weight of the bird.

- Higher metabolism, temperature, blood pressure, and a hyperactive heart contribute to the bird's success.

- A remarkable system of respiration where the hollow bones provide an air sac system, providing buoyancy, a reservoir for respiration and an air conditioner.

- Air flows into the lungs in only one direction, providing a continuous supply of oxygen.

- Other features: streamlining, retractable landing gear, camouflage, migration navigation, and hibernation.

It is unreasonable to suggest that the hummingbird "developed" all of these features as a product of evolution gradually over millions of years. Time and chance cannot produce such design and order. Only God can!

Fishy Stories!

The Anableps is a fish that spends his life on the surface of the water. Although he is a rather small fish, he poses a big problem for evolutionists. You see, his eyes are divided in half, the top designed for seeing in air out of the water, and the bottom for seeing below the surface of the water.[8] What were the transitional forms like? What kind of evolutionary "pressure" could cause half of an eye to gradually evolve to see out of the water?

Anableps Eye

The Archer Fish

The Archer fish overcomes a problem in sea to air ballistics. He squirts water at his prey, which are bugs and flies. His mouth has a built in groove that channels the water like a squirt gun. But the biggest problem is his aim. He has to overcome the refractive difference from water to air in order to accurately hit his prey.[9] If you ever looked at a spoon in a glass of water, you would understand the problem. The refractive quality of water makes it appear to be broken in half. Again we marvel at God's design.

A Fish Goes Fishing!

Consider the angler fish, who has an appendage dangling in front of his mouth that attracts other fish, and when the prey gets close enough, chomp!

The angler fish lives at great depths and has to handle a lot of water pressure. But the biggest problem for evolutionists is the fact that the male of the species doesn't eat! By an amazing process, he attaches himself to the female, and the bloodstreams of the two merge! Imagine the changes the male would have had to go through in order to evolve this gradually over a period of millions of years!

Like the angler fish, the decoy fish also lures its prey by means of a bait. One of its fins resembles a small fish standing out in contrast to the rest of the body, which blends in well with the environment. The prey, as it approaches the decoy fish, sees only the fishy looking fin and does not realize that it is part of a much bigger fish.

The Decoy Fish

Flytrap Claptrap

Imagine the fun our Creator had in making the Venus Flytrap, the carnivorous plant. What a problem for an evolutionist this creates! On the surface of the trap are trigger hairs causing an action potential similar to a nerve response, closing the trap.[10] The plant then secretes digestive juices and the dying insect gives off weak solutions of sodium and ammonium ions, causing the trap to close more firmly.

In order for a Venus Flytrap to be functional, the plant must have in place a full-formed trap mechanism complete with trigger hairs, digestive glands, living bars, and action potential response before any insects could be trapped. Also, the trap would have to have the capability of responding to the sodium ions secreted by the dying ants and flies so that the proper narrowing and digestion could occur.

Recent research regarding the flytraps has found that ants are a more common prey than flies. Scientists formerly believed that a scent was secreted by the trap, attracting the insects. This idea was ruled out after intensive observation, finding that the most frequently trapped insects were either poor fliers, clumsy fliers or non-flying forms that walk into the trap accidentally.

Another result of this study is the conclusion that the flytraps do quite well, grow, produce flowers, set seed, and fully propagate without ever eating a single insect. Why would such a structure "evolve"? Since there is no significant advantage to the trap forming by itself, I would rather believe that God created it as a curiosity.

Evolution Croaks!

Fossils of supposedly ancient frogs show that frogs have always resembled frogs. This is one of the problems evolutionists face, that many modern animals are very much like their fossil counterparts, with no evolutionary change apparent over the imagined millions of years. Gerald H. Duffett[11] outlines a method of linking together vital functions of the frog as proof of creation. He provides detailed diagrams linking together these functions, showing that no single entity is fully functional alone and that other entities are required to make each entity fully functional. The following is a summary of his "linkological" evaluation of the frog.

List of entities:

1. Air
2. Tiny lungs
3. No trachea
4. No neck
5. Undifferentiated Vertebrae
6. No thorax
7. No abdomen
8. No diaphragm
9. No ribs
10. Pectoral girdle shields heart and absorbs shock
11. No rib muscles
12. Urostyle
13. Hind legs for leaping
14. No larynx
15. Glottal epithelial flaps
16. Vocal pouches
17. Croak
18. Single Ventricle
19. Atria receive oxygenated blood
20. Cutaneous respiration
21. Amplexus
22. Fore limbs
23. Highly vascular skin
24. Mucus
25. Nuptial pads on males
26. Poikilothermy: cold-blooded
27. Hibernation
28. Low ambient temperature
29. Webbed feet
30. Pond water
31. External fertilization
32. Gamete release
33. Identification of opposite sex
34. No external auditory meatus
35. Tympanic membrane on head surface
36. No air under water
37. No need for a secondary palate
38. Nostril closes
39. Vomerine teeth on roof of mouth
40. Eyeballs are retractable to aid swallowing

From this list of entities, Dr. Duffett compiles an entity link list connecting each of these features together into a matrix of interrelationships. The existence of such a network of links is clear evidence of a creator! Complex systems such as this do not come about by chance. From the above list of features, he compiles an exhaustive list of over 60 different links where each feature cannot exist without the other.

Here are some examples:

From:	To:	
1	2	Air being less dense than water would not allow frog to dive for cover if lungs were not small.
1	20	Air diffuses through skin to enter blood capillaries.
2	3	Tiny lungs are not only too puny to have a reinforced windpipe leading to them, but they are subsidiary to skin.
2	19	Atria receive blood equally oxygenated because skin is as efficient as a respiratory surface as tiny lungs.
2	30	The much greater density of water compared with air prevents frog from carrying large lung full of from pond surface to pond bottom.
3	4	No point in having a neck if no trachea is present.
8	6	No diaphragm so no boundary in trunk to separate thorax from abdomen. Therefore, no thorax.
8	7	No diaphragm so no boundary in trunk to separate thorax from abdomen. Therefore, no abdomen.
13	10	After jumping with hind limbs, pectoral girdle absorbs shock of landing on hard ground.
14	40	No larynx means that swallowing must therefore be performed by muscles pulling eyeballs into head to push food in esophagus.
20	19	Skin respiration causes blood leaving skin to be oxygenated as blood leaves tiny lungs.
20	23	Skin respiration is possible because that organ is richly supplied with blood vessels.
20	30	Oxygen dissolved in water can diffuse into skin both when frog is in the pond and when frog is on dry land provided that its skin remains moist.
23	19	Rich blood supply to skin ensures that oxygen diffuses into frog.
30	34	Frogs would become deaf if water entered their ear holes so they have no external auditory meatus on their heads.
37	40	No eye socket bones and no secondary palate allow eyeballs to be retracted by muscles and so help push food into esophagus.

Mr. Duffett's "linkological" approach illustrates the thorough systems analysis God used when He created the frog. It is important for us to use an approach like this when evaluating any creature in nature. Interdependence between entities can be documented through this linkological evaluation, showing that one system cannot exist without the other. This requires instant creation of these entities in order for functionality to exist. The probability of even two of these entities occurring by chance independently in the same organism at the same time is extremely remote. But the frog exhibits over 60 such interdependent entities!

Creation Wins By A Neck

Have you ever wondered why the giraffe's brain doesn't explode when he stoops to get a drink of water? Or, why he doesn't pass out when he raises his head back up again? It's because God has specially created valves in his neck which close off the enormous flow of blood needed to raise it to the giraffe's great height.

The giraffe has a powerful heart almost two feet long to make sure the blood supply gets to his brain. But if he did not have the special valves in his arteries which regulate his blood supply, his brains would explode under the pressure. Also, there is a special sponge underneath the giraffe's brain which absorbs the last pump of blood. Now, when he raises back up, that sponge squeezes that oxygenated blood into his brain, the valves open up, and he doesn't pass out.

Now, could this mechanism have evolved? No way! If the first giraffe had a long neck and two foot long heart, but no mechanism to regulate it, when he first stooped to get a drink of water, he would have blown his mind. Then, after he had blown his mind, he would have thought to himself, "I need to evolve valves in my arteries to regulate this!" No, he would have been dead! The giraffe's long neck couldn't have evolved; it needed to be completely functional in the first place.

I'll Scratch Your Back; You Scratch Mine!

Structured throughout nature is interdependence. In

I Corinthians 12, we have the illustration of the body of Christ and its members functioning as an organism. Likewise, organisms in nature need each other to fulfil their roles.

A curiosity I studied in microbiology class was a microorganism called *Mixotricha Paradoxa* that lives in the gut of Australian termites. When it was first discovered, it looked as if it was covered with a bunch of curly hairs. Looking at it closer, it was revealed that these were not hairs at all, but spirochetes, which were a totally different type of microorganism. On the *Mixotricha*, there were bumps or appendages where the spirochetes attached, and a bacillus which lodged on the other side of the bump. The spirochetes provided a means of locomotion for the entire colony of microorganisms. They are three totally different germs that decided to live together in a community.

So, what you have is an interdependence between a large microorganism, a spirochete, a bacillus, an Australian

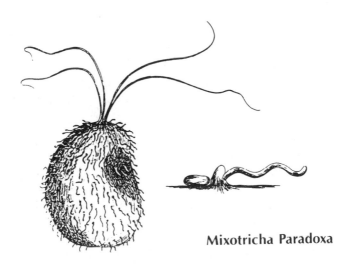

Mixotricha Paradoxa

termite, and even the trees the termite feed upon. I suppose if you are an evolutionist, you would have to believe that at one point in time they formed a committee and decided to all work together; the *Mixotricha* "developing" bumps where the spirochetes could bury their heads and behind which the bacillus could hide; all of whom "decided" to live in the gut of a termite.

Interdependence and ecology are problems for evolutionists. These principles demonstrate that there are delicate balances between all of the different species on the earth and that each is dependent upon the other. Which evolved first, a species or the food it feeds upon?

Reproduction provides an illustration of the problem that interdependence causes for evolutionists. The old "Which came first, the chicken or the egg" dilemma may cause a lot of laughter, but it still doesn't make the problem go away. For those who believe the Biblical account of creation, the answer is simple: it was the chicken originally created by God.

I like to look for telltale statements evolutionists make. For example, they say that "the aardvark is the only surviving example of an obscure mammalian genus."[12] Translation: they can't find any other animal enough like it to classify it, nor can they find any fossilized transitional forms. With a pig's snout, donkey ears, and sharp claws for burrowing, it is unique. The same holds true for the panda and the giant anteater. They have a combination of features that defy the traditional rules of classification.

Creationists, since they don't have to explain transitions from one species to another, have the simplest explanation for the origin of life. Those who reject the Biblical explanation are now having a more difficult time in the face of strongly negative evidence against evolution. Some scientists like Frances Crick and Fred Hoyle, unwilling to accept a Christian perspective, believe the concept that life was imported to earth by space aliens or on a meteorite. Others are adhering to the "hopeful monster" theory or the so-called "punctuated equilibrium" theory, the idea that massive changes took place all at once. In effect they believe that a reptile mutated, laid an egg and a bird hatched out. But it would have to happen twice in the same place to provide a mate for the new emerging species.

As a way to solidify the creationist position, we contemplate the scenario for the theory of evolution: examine the animal as it exists today in its environment, and visualize the supposed gradual "adaptation" from one environment to another. Analyze each feature of the animal and show how these features came to be. For the most part, evolutionists can only come up with speculation, and little fossil evidence to support it.

For review, let us examine the assumptions of evolution, which are all, by their nature, incapable of experimental verification. All of these involve a certain series of presumed events in the past. Even if it were possible to duplicate these experimentally, it does not mean that they occurred at all. Therefore, since evolution is beyond direct experimental verification, no honest man can state with certainty that the world is the product of an evolutionary process. The assumptions of evolution are listed as follows:

- Non-living things gave rise to living things (spontaneous generation).

- Spontaneous generation occurred only once, and did not repeat at any time.

- Viruses, bacteria, plants and animals are all interrelated; all from the same source.

- The protozoa gave rise to the metazoa.

- The invertebrates are interrelated.

- The invertebrates gave rise to the vertebrates.

- The vertebrates and fish gave rise to the amphibians, the amphibians to the reptiles, and the reptiles to the birds and mammals.

Evolutionists would ask us to take these assumptions and believe them in faith. "After all, how could all of these scientists who have spent dedicated years in research be so wrong?" Creationists have no quarrel with the data and the facts found by scientists. What we disagree with are the conclusions drawn from this data. Important facts conflicting with the theory of evolution have been glossed over, ignored, or thrown out as "experimental error". Scientific data is subject to interpretation. That is the function of theories. Theories must be revised to fit the facts, and if a theory is irreconcilable to the facts, discard it..

SCRIPTURE REFERENCES

Psalm 104
Job 39

QUESTIONS FOR STUDY

1. Describe briefly the logic used in this chapter to show how certain animals do not fit the theory of evolution.

2. List several of these animals and their unique traits that confound evolutionists.

3. What are some of the major environmental transitions the theory of evolution has to explain?

4. Would "transitional forms" between animals in existence today have survived?

5. Using the same indirect proof logic, describe an animal not mentioned in this chapter that presents the same kind of problems for evolutionists.

VI. PROTEINS, DNA, AND THE CELL

To understand the origin of life, we examine life's basic building blocks, the interrelationships between them, and their origin. There have been many "origin of life" experiments trying to duplicate a scenario where life could have arisen on the earth millions of years ago by chance. These experiments have ultimately one goal: to justify a materialistic philosophy that excludes God. But, the very nature of their experiments proves the opposite, that it takes creative intervention to produce the building blocks of life!

Is it possible for atoms to materialize, organize themselves, and combine to form living things without the influence of an intelligent creator? We have considered the effects of the second law of thermodynamics, which shows that the natural tendency in the universe is toward decay, disorganization and death. In the physics and chemistry of life, is that law reversed? If we use the laws of probability and chance, we can show what it would take for life to form independently of God.

The Improbability of Probability

To understand probability, let us look at a few examples. The probability of a flipped coin coming up heads is 1 chance out of 2. What is the chance of three coins coming up heads? It is one out of 2 X 2 X 2 or eight. As we increase the number of coins flipped, the probability of getting all heads decreases rapidly. With ten coins, the probability is 1 in 1024. With 20 coins, it is 1 in 524,288.

The Left-Handed Amino Acid Dilemma

Let us now apply the principles of probability to the problem of origin of life. Proteins are an important family of molecules that make up life. They are gigantic in comparison to ordinary chemicals found outside life. Typically, a protein is 400 to 1000 times larger and more complex than the molecules that make up gasoline. A protein is a polymer, which is a chain of components all linked together. We call these links in the chain amino acids.

If you chemically build amino acids in a test tube, they will form into equal amounts of "right handed" and "left handed" isomers. This refers to the three dimensional shape of the molecules. Chemically, the right handed and left handed forms react the same, and are indistinguishable apart from their three dimensional orientation. The two forms are mirror images of each other.

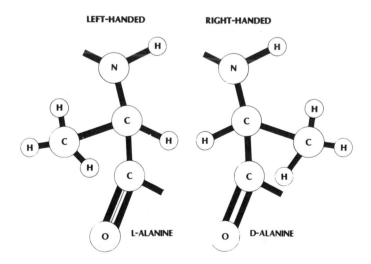

There are twenty different amino acids used as building blocks in proteins. The sequence of the amino acids and the three dimensional shape determine the function of the protein. Therefore, let us look at what it would take to create a functional protein or enzyme.

A typical protein is made up of a chain of 445 left-handed amino acids. No protein found in nature contains right handed amino acids. Though origin of life experiments produce equal mixtures of both, all proteins use only the left-handed variety. Therefore, in order for the original protein to be formed, all amino acids used out of the original mixture needed to be left-handed.

We can now apply the laws of probability to this. The chances of an average protein consisting of 445 amino acids forming by chance is one chance out of 2^{410} or 10^{123} (35 of the amino acids would be glycine, which is symmetrical).[1]

To illustrate the magnitude of this impossibility, let's have a contest. Suppose we give a snail moving at the speed of one inch every million years the task of moving the entire earth atom by atom over to the other side of the universe and back.

Then, imagine the length of time it takes light to travel one millimeter, and a million proteins forming in that length of time hoping to form one protein with all left-handed amino acids. Guess what! The snail would win, many millions of times over before even one left-handed protein would be formed!

Presume now that we can make amino acids ambidextrous for the moment and ignore this problem for the evolutionists' sake. We now have a problem making sure that the amino acids are in the right order to give the protein its function. Each amino acid has a characteristic that forms weak bonds, giving the protein its three dimensional shape. It is this shape that gives the protein its activity in living systems.

If we disturb a protein with an outside force such as

heat, acid, or any other abnormal environment, the three dimensional shape of the protein will be upset, and it will lose its activity. When this happens, we say the protein is *denatured.* Therefore, a protein may have all its amino acids left-handed and in proper sequence and still be useless because the three dimensional shape is not correct.

Disulfide Bridges

Hydrogen Bonding

Hydrophobic

Ionic

Vanderwaals Attractions

Weak Bonds Determine Shape and Activity of Enzyme

There are twenty amino acids that make up the basic building blocks of the protein. The order is very important, like the code of a computer program, or a sentence in a book. If just one amino acid is out of sequence, it changes the entire structure of the protein, just like changing a word in a sentence.

This is the effect of a mutation. It weakens the protein's function, usually to the point where it no longer does its job. The origin of disease is simple, it is a departure from the perfect creation of God caused by mutations. Mutations are a degenerative process and not the driving force evolutionists seek to explain the origin of life.

Let us assume in spite of the incredible odds that we now have a protein meeting every requirement, with left-handed amino acids, proper amino acid sequence and three dimensional structure. The next problem to face is configuring the least number of proteins, needed with DNA and associated molecules to form a living cell.

Scientists estimate that 238 proteins would be the absolute minimum number that would be needed to form life.[2] Is it possible to bring together that many proteins and interrelate them in such a way to continuously process food and energy? A problem in doing this is even if we concentrated the right proteins together in the same place at once, they still would have to be configured in the proper structure in order for life to exist.

Coppedge, in his book, *Evolution: Possible or Impossible*, makes several probability calculations concerning life coming about by chance. Giving evolution all kinds of concessions, he comes up with the probability for the first cell to evolve by accident as one chance in 10^{29345}. It would take an 80 page book just to print that number. In comparison, the number of inches across the known universe is 10^{28}. From these figures, you can be certain that the evolution of the cell is impossible![3]

Some have thought that viruses are precursors to living cells, but to reproduce, viruses need living cells as hosts! So even if a virus happened to appear by chance, it would have been the last unless there was a cell nearby whose reproductive mechanism it could exploit.

More Left-Handed Right-Handed Problems

Found throughout life are other examples of where life prefers one choice out of many equally possible chemical designs. Sugars occur naturally only in the right handed form in life, yet have the same synthesis problems that amino acids have.

Researchers conducted an experiment synthesizing protein-like chains using equal mixtures of left handed and right handed amino acids, then introduced them into a cell. The cell excised out the right handed variety, often replacing them with the left handed type![4]

Lipids present an even worse problem in that life uses only the cis configuration though the trans configuration is chemically more stable. That is why if you make lipids in the test tube, you will get much more yield of the trans variety rather than the cis.[5]

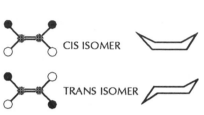

CIS ISOMER

TRANS ISOMER

Examples of CIS and TRANS configurations

Interrelationships Between Cell Components

The cell has a unique manufacturing process that has a standardized way of mass producing all the components needed to sustain life. The DNA molecule is the master template, the pattern for all the components that make up life. The RNA molecule is produced from this master template. This in turn becomes an assembly line. Each set of three nucleotides on the RNA molecule is a code read by another large protein complex known as a ribosome. The ribosome proceeds down the RNA molecule, reading every three nucleotides to decide what amino acid to place in the growing protein chain.

The interesting part of this whole process is that the product, a protein, is necessary for each reaction along the chain to proceed. The DNA molecule cannot form without its corresponding enzyme, DNA polymerase. Yet, DNA polymerase is a product of this manufacturing process. Enzymes also catalyze the other reactions occurring in the process. Each cell component has its own niche and purpose, without which the cell would die.

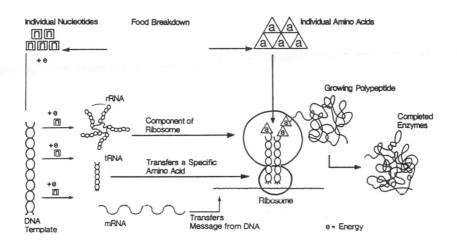

Therefore, this whole process cannot take place until all the components are together, integrated to the point where they react with one another properly. This is truly a design by God. One marvels at the systems engineering required to put into place such a complex manufacturing process.

A systems integrator can tell you that it takes painstaking design and attention to detail to get even two or three programs or computer systems to work together. Suppose we created one computer program, and altered it one letter, command, or section at a time at random to produce another computer program. Would we eventually end up with an integrated system? Experience tells us otherwise. So even if we started with DNA, RNA or a protein fully functional, and one of them was able to catalyze reactions all by itself or replicate itself, it would not explain the integrated systems we observe in the cell. Random processes cannot produce information and function. Yet, when we observe life, we see perfect system integration, except where it is damaged by mutation.

Suppose a scientist were to break open the contents of dead cells and place the remains in a flask. With meticulous work, he might be able to get a few of the reactions to go for a moment, but he would not be able to resurrect life in the cells. If he subjected them to ultraviolet light or zapped them with lightning, it would cause more damage. If he left it alone for a length of time, the molecules would decay, not evolve. Yet, supposedly, all of the chemicals needed for life are there!

The idea of "cellular ecology" reflects not only scientific principles but Christian principles. In the body of Christ, each part has a function and purpose, none of which is more important than the other, and without which life would cease. Similarly, the cell functions the same way, the body functions the same way, and the environment functions the same way. Divide the cell, and the cell will die. Divide the body, and the body will die. Cut off a portion of the environment, and the environment will die.[6]

Induction and Repression

A function of enzymes is to regulate the normal processes occurring in the organism such as digestion and the production of energy. This regulation takes place through the systems of *induction* and *repression.* Repression takes place when the product of a reaction binds to the enzyme, forcing it into an inactive state, effectively shutting off the reaction when enough product is produced. Co-repression acts similarly, but here the product binds to the repressor, which then turns on the repression process.[7] Induction takes place when the product of one reaction starts up another. How could such processes originate, except by a wise creator?

Let us review now the conditions necessary for life to come about by chance through the process of evolution. The following is a list of the steps that would need to take place.

1. First, the chemicals needed to produce life had to be available in the atmosphere to make both amino acids and nucleotides.

2. To make both amino acids and nucleotides, an atmosphere without oxygen is necessary.

3. Amino acids would have to be purified in the left handed form.

4. The amino acids would have to be linked up in a chain in the right sequence to form an active protein.

5. A corresponding DNA gene would have to be synthesized with the necessary code to produce the protein.

6. The protein manufacturing process would have to be in place with transfer RNA, messenger RNA, and ribosomes for the protein to be mass produced.

7. The enzyme, DNA polymerase, would have to be available in order for DNA to form.

8. One enzyme is not enough to sustain life. In order for life to function, there would need to be more than 200 enzymes with their corresponding DNA, RNA, and manufacturing systems functioning together in a system.

Mutations Can Be Hazardous To Your Health

The theory of evolution is heavily dependent upon mutations to explain the vast variety of plants and animals. Let's examine this idea to find out if beneficial mutations really occur and whether it is a valid explanation for evolution.

Biochemists have identified several mechanisms where cells repair damaged genes. The case that is best understood is where a gene is damaged by ultraviolet radiation when two adjacent thymine links in the DNA molecule bind together. If left unrepaired, this would kill the cell. A series of enzymes especially designed to eat away this part of the DNA replace them with a new, correct set of nucleotides. But if this repair mechanism does not work, a backup biochemical pathway takes over and repairs the problem.

It is this secondary pathway that may cause a mutation by replacing the thymines with another nucleotide. This normally does not occur. Consider this: what is the origin of these repair processes? Truly, it cannot be a product of an accident. When a mutation occurs, it is usually due to a mistake in repair of damaged genes, or a mistake in the reading of the DNA template. Such mutations are either recessive, nonfunctional, lethal, repaired, or weeded out.

What would it take for someone to build a machine where if anything went wrong, repair processes would occur automatically? Suppose also, if something went wrong with the automatic repair process in that machine, a backup mechanism took over the repair process. I know of no such machine in existence devised by man, yet evolutionists believe that this process came about by chance in life. I would like to see car manufacturers come up with process that will automatically repair blown gaskets, smash-ups, engine failures, and replace worn parts. That process is already built into life!

Another type of mutation occurs when strings of nucleotides replace sections of a DNA molecule. This would be like inserting one sentence or paragraph at random in this book, changing its meaning. If that were to occur, would it make sense? Of course not, unless some intelligent person was guiding the selection of the paragraph. Natural selection is a weeding out of information that is not useful to life, and cannot produce complex systems. I believe instead in **devolution**, which is the decay and death from a perfect creation marred by sin.

To believe that mutations are the origin of all the diversity in life is to believe that random chance results in a beneficial change. Evolutionists themselves do not believe that. Otherwise, I'd like them to submit to an experiment. How would you like to have your genes randomized?

All right, evolutionists, line up! How many volunteers do we have who want to irradiate their genes in the hope that somehow it will result in a higher degree of evolution? Perhaps you might evolve lungs that will breathe polluted air or a body that will resist polluted water? Would you be ready to undergo such an experiment?

Enzymes

Another example of God's creative power is in the design of enzymes. Enzymes are proteins, used as a catalyst in chemical reactions in the body. Enzymes speed up reactions by acting as a machine to digest or break apart certain chemicals. The chemical or food particle attaches to the enzyme, bending into the position where it will react the best.

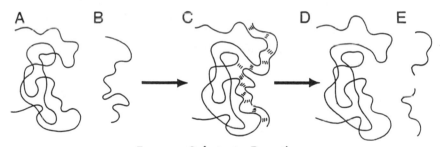

Enzyme-Substrate Reaction
A: Enzyme   B: Substrate   C: Reaction   D: Enzyme   E: End Product

The processes of induction and repression regulate the rate and amount of digestion that takes place. Depending on the amount of energy and food needed, processes turn on and off like machines.

How does an evolutionist explain how this process came about? I have never seen anyone attempt to give an explanation. The problem of interrelationships is simply ignored. Chance cannot produce these intricate relationships. At the molecular level, as there is between animals, these interrelationships occur throughout all parts of the organism, much like a microscopic ecology. Each piece has its function, a job to do. Death would result if any mistakes occur in these operations.

Art F. Poettcker outlines a list of seventeen problems evolutionists cannot answer concerning mutations, genes, and life at the molecular level:[8]

1. Structural changes in chromosomes are most often deleterious and at best only produce variation within a kind.

2. Observed mutations have resulted in changes only in existing traits.

3. Mutations are harmful or useless.

4. The mutation rate is very low.

5. Homozygous mutants would tend to eliminate a species.

6. The more complex an organism, the less chance there is for mutations to occur of advantage even under new environmental conditions.

7. Any mutation is likely to upset the delicate gene complex.

8. The origin of dominance does not have a suitable explanation.

9. Reverse mutations add to the problem of time required for mutations.

10. Polyploidy is an evolutionary dead end.

11. Chromosome number and DNA content vary widely between alleged evolutionary levels.

12. Even allowing for beneficial mutations, natural selection may be too slow to account for alleged evolution.

13. Too rapid a rate of natural selection may eliminate the entire population.

14. Most favorable mutations are eliminated from a population.

15. Genetic drift operates opposite to selection.

16. Natural selection limits its effect to populations.

17. Mutation and natural selection do not have a means to operate upon chemical molecules.

Any one of these problems is enough to cause us to think twice about evolution at the molecular level. The scientific principles of genetics, when you get down to the facts, demonstrate creation much more than they do evolution.

Let's look at what happens during the healing process. I believe that natural healing is **supernatural healing** taken for granted! The reason I believe this is when you examine what takes place when a cut finger heals, or a virus or microorganism invades the body, you find amazing pro-

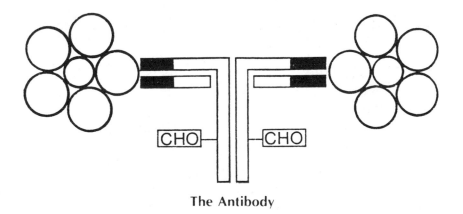

The Antibody

cesses at work to quickly remedy the problem. If you take a sledge hammer to your car, do you expect it to undent itself? Then why do we take healing for granted, not acknowledging God's intervention when we experience it, even with an ordinary cut?

Consider the antibody. It has a fixed chemical makeup that gives it its form, but it has ends with a variable amino acid structure that change to attach to foreign bodies and like a microbial bouncer, the antibody throws out the offender. How does the theory of evolution explain the origin of healing and antibodies? Without the purpose of God's creative power behind it, it doesn't make sense.

The Cleansing Blood

God gives us a perfect illustration of salvation through the shedding of the blood of Christ at Calvary. Some people do not understand the meaning of this; after all, doesn't blood stain things, not cleanse? But when we look at the function of blood in the body, we discover that it does act as a cleansing agent, ridding the body of toxins and wastes. If you apply a tourniquet around your wrist for a few minutes, you will experience the discomfort that follows the buildup of these toxins in your tissues, since the blood cannot carry them away.

After the blood picks up the waste products in the body, it delivers them to the kidney, which is the most efficient waste disposal machine on the earth. The kidney filters these waste products, breaking them down to be recycled if possible or ejected. What the blood does for the human body is a perfect illustration of what the blood of Christ does for the body of Christ. It cleanses us from all sin; again defined as the waste, poisons and junk our lives produce.

Look at life's processes and marvel! Just because we can describe them, it doesn't mean we've explained their origin! Instead, we need to acknowledge God's hand in their creation.

SCRIPTURE REFERENCES

Isaiah 53:4-5
I Corinthians 12
Hebrews 11:3

QUESTIONS FOR STUDY

1. If we filled the entire earth with amino acids and they formed proteins as fast as possible, would there be enough time in the "history" of the universe for life to form? Why?

2. How does each molecule in a cell, each cell within an organism, each organism in an environment relate to one another?

3. How do these relationships apply to the relationships we have in the body of Christ?

4. What is the origin of repair mechanisms, and how do they relate to healing?

5. What conditions would have to be on the earth in order for life to come about by chance? Are those conditions realistic? Why?

6. What are the odds of having one protein form with all left-handed amino acids by chance?

VII. THE STARS AND PLANETS

Recent discoveries of NASA space missions have created "astronomical" problems for evolutionists. NASA engineers designed the lunar lander with spindly legs so that it could land in space dust they presumed accumulated on the moon over billions of years. One scientist predicted that the dust levels would be over a hundred feet thick, based upon the amount of cosmic dust and rate of erosion.[1] Isaac Asimov also believed that the thickness of dust may be dozens of feet thick.[2] When the astronauts landed on the moon, the dust was less than an inch thick. Using the observed rate of dust accumulation, this is evidence for a young moon.

The currently accepted uniformitarian theories on the origin and age of lunar craters can be challenged by observing the rate they wear down. Over long periods of time, solids behave like liquids, with expansion and contraction causing the surface of the moon to "flow" until the surface becomes level. Since lunar craters still exist, it shows their relative youth. Morton, Slusher, and Mandock use viscosity studies to show that lunar craters cannot be more than a few thousand to a few million years.[3]

The Big Bang: A Lot of Noise?

There are three different non-creationist theories of the origin of the universe: the **Big Bang Theory**, the **Steady State Theory** and the **Pulsating Universe Theory**. Evolutionists promote these theories with impressive mathematical detail involving lots of premises and speculations. The problem is that each theory begs the question, and by assumption rules out a supernatural origin. If the universe is running down, somehow the laws of physics and thermodynamics got reversed to "wind" up the universe.

Has astronomical observation produced evidence that cannot be explained by the creation model? I have to admire the imagination of non-creationists, and their ability to extrapolate data back billions of years to produce a model of the universe. Yet, even if everything did fit a mathematical and scientific model, since we cannot observe, test, or repeat it, there is no proof that it occurred that way. The creation model is by far the simplest.

We can reveal the motivation behind the "big bang" theory by examining the assumptions. If evolutionists do not allow for the possibility that God created the universe, it is not surprising what conclusions they will come to. The way they think, if it "could have possibly" happened that way, they therefore don't have to believe in God.

Creationist Cosmologies

If we assume an ancient cosmos, it would not necessarily violate the integrity and accuracy of scripture. But, given the record of evolutionary assumptions, it is unwise to dismiss the possibility that the creation of the cosmos took place at the same time as the creation of the earth and solar system. Let us review   assumptions evolutionists make in their theories:

1. Light travels in straight lines.
2. The speed of light is constant.
3. The Doppler effect causes the red shift.
4. The distance of stars can be determined by the Hubble constant and comparisons of star cluster size.
5. The second law of thermodynamics was reversed, or began at the big bang.
6. Time, space, and distance are consistent throughout the universe.
7. Space is a vacuum.

One creationist view of the universe explores the idea that the universe is not Euclidian in nature, but curved. If light travels in arcs over vast distances, the source of the light would appear to be much further away than it actually is because of triangulation problems.[4]

The vast distance of stars may then be apparent distances of images, and not the actual distance of the light source. Triangulation distance measurements have an outward limit of 60 to 400 light years. This is due to the limits of the base of the triangle, which is the diameter of earth's rotation around the sun six months apart, or 186 million miles. Beyond 400 light years, evolutionists rely upon comparisons of the magnitudes of stars, and calculations based on the Hubble constant. The Hubble constant is derived from the doppler shift. The question is, why do the most distant stars show the highest red shift? Another explanation could be that gravity fields and dust, both plentiful in space, could cause the same effect.[5] Could this be a better explanation?

Evolutionists are hoping that the nearsighted Hubble telescope with its new corrective lenses will provide the answers someday.

Other creationists have suggested that the speed of light has decreased over time, or decays over long distances. The "tired light" theory, as it is sometimes called, would explain a young universe with an apparent great age.[6] Recent works by Morton and Setterfield have attempted to show historical measurements of the speed of light to be slightly higher than they are today.[7,8] The results of these studies have raised a spirited debate, since to preserve conservation of energy, other "constants" also would have to vary: permeability of free space, atomic rest mass, Planck's constant, Gyromagnetic ratio, the radioactive decay constant, and thermal conductivity of a substance. Another model concerning the speed of light assumes that in the beginning, the speed of light was infinite, instantaneously decreasing to its present speed.

Light is an electromagnetic disturbance. If God created mature electromagnetic fields the same time He created the stars, He could have created the light from the distant stars in route at the instant of creation. Therefore the light from stars appearing to be millions of light years away may have been created in route only a few thousand years ago.

Evidence For Youth: Comets

The rate of space dust accumulation and the existence of lunar craters are evidence for a young solar system. Other bodies in the solar system that cannot be very old are comets. Comets disintegrate very quickly in comparison to the long expanses of time required by evolution. The breakdown of several comets has been observed over the course of history. An example is Belia's comet, which one year split into two comets, then on successive returns broke into pieces, becoming a meteor shower. If comets and the solar system were formed at the same time, it would show that the solar system is young.

Therefore, most astronomers have to assume that the origin of comets is separate from the origin of the solar system, and develop elaborate theories for their capture by planetary perturbations.

Calculations for a short period comet of its loss of mass in each orbit show that they probably cannot last more than 10,000 years. Furthermore, the same perturbations that might cause them to be captured in orbit also would eject them out of the solar system under the influence of Jupiter and the other planets. If the solar system is as old as 4.5 billion years, there would be few comets.

Io

One of the most fascinating events of this century was the missions of the Pioneer and Voyager space probes, and the amazing photographs they transmitted to earth. From the findings of these missions, the discovery of active volcanoes on the Galilean moon of Io produced the most amazement and controversy.[9] If that moon was millions of years old, it would have cooled by now. Why would there be so much volcanic activity on this moon if it was really millions of years old? The photographs sent back by Voyager portrayed a "hell" of molten lava and an active, erupting volcano spewing ejecta hundreds of miles above the surface of the moon.

The problem of active volcanoes is not limited to Io, but also contradicts the idea of an old earth. If the earth is really billions of years old, it would be expected that it would have cooled by now. According to calculations based upon cooling rates and the size of the Io and the earth, there should be no volcanoes. Therefore, evolutionists have to come up with an explanation for the internal heat generated by both the earth and Io.

One such explanation is that the earth creates heat through a dynamo effect caused by friction of molten magma within the earth's core. For Io, they postulated that the gravitational pull between the various Galilean moons causes friction and heat. Even those explanations do not account for the loss of that heat over millions of years.

Saturn

The flight of the Voyager spacecraft revealed many odd things about the planet Saturn. Finger like projections or spokes stretch across the B ring and are slightly darker than the ring itself. Also found were eccentric rings, and some rings were fatter on one side than another. The problem with these explanations is that they defy known laws of orbital mechanics. Theoretically spokes in the rings would not form since the closer ring would move faster than the outer rings. The spokes should tear apart.

The moons of Saturn are heavily cratered, which many have pointed to as evidence for recent catastrophe. Mimas, the innermost moon, exhibits the largest impact crater known in the solar system. Its diameter is one third that of the moon. It seems that freezing and expanding would soon eliminate the craters on these moons if they were millions of years old. Yet Mimas has extensive cratering, so much that to make more, you would have to make craters on top of craters.

The doctrines of evolution are based upon uniformitarianism, the idea that all processes observed today have remained the same over millions of years and have occurred gradually. The evidence is to the contrary in the solar system.

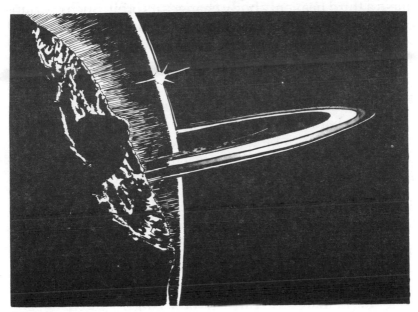

Mimas

Stellar Evolution

Astronomers have an elaborate theory regarding the origin of the stars that establishes the age of each star according to its size and chemical makeup. According to this theory, the star undergoes changes from its initial contraction from interstellar gas, through stages of intermediate sizes, expansion to gigantism, finally to collapse, becoming a white dwarf. Each stage is supposed to take millions of years.

A problem with the stellar evolution theory is binary star systems containing stars of different evolutionary ages. Most of the binary star systems involve two or more stars of different stellar "ages" revolving around each other. This does not make sense, because the physics involved in one star capturing another would have to involve a third star perturbing one of them. If two bodies encounter one another, their orbits follow hyperbolic paths, not elliptical, unless a third heavenly body changes its orbit. Such encounters would be extremely rare. The same dynamics would catapult them out of orbit.

The most likely situation is that the stars in a binary star system would have formed simultaneously. Since there are an abundance of binary star systems, it is easier to believe that the stellar "ages" were the result of the star's original gas content than to believe that they were formed by star capture. Despite size and chemical makeup, the best conclusion is that binary stars would have to be the same age.

The Decay of the Earth's Magnetic Field

Dr. Thomas G. Barnes has prepared a technical monograph describing the earth's magnetic field in detail, and measurement of its strength over the last 130 years.[10] According to Dr. Barnes, these measurements show that the magnetic field of the earth is decaying in intensity and strength at a measurable rate.

The graph of this decay shows that the half-life of the earth's magnetic moment is 1400 years, which is very short on a historical point of view. One interesting aspect of this observation is that we can extrapolate the strength of the magnetic field backward along that curve. His calculations show that if the earth were more than 10,000 years old, that it would have had enough magnetic energy to be a star.

If the earth's magnetic field was much stronger in the past, it would have reduced the production of carbon-14 in the atmosphere. Carbon-14 dating is based upon the assumption that the rate of carbon-14 production in the atmosphere has been constant. The net effect would be that dates previously thought to be old would be greatly reduced in age.

A high magnetic field could have provided a protective effect as part of the environment before the flood, shielding the earth from cosmic radiation. Researchers conducted experiments where they kept mice in an environment with a high magnetic field surrounding them. These mice lived much longer, were fatter, larger, and healthier than the control mice. If the magnetic field of the earth was stronger before the flood, this could perhaps help to explain the long ages of the patriarchs, and the abundance of large animals in the fossil record.

Evolutionists believe that a series of magnetic field reversals took place and that the Earth's core acts as a dynamo to fuel the energy for the magnetic field. Dr. Barnes shows that the evidence for this idea is weak because the data does not give conclusive evidence of reversals. He points out that Cowling proved that it is not possible for fluid motions to generate a magnetic field with axial symmetry (such as the dipole field of the Earth).

UFO's

Unidentified flying objects have been the subject of speculations concerning evolution and the origin of life upon the earth. Some non-creationists, like Sir Fred Hoyle and Frances Crick, have resorted to this explanation, faced with the impossible odds of the chemical origin of life. Unwilling to embrace the Biblical supernatural God, they create a super-technological one.

But, the *Chariots of the Gods* theory popularized by Erich von Daniken years ago, and similar ideas published recently by Sir Fred Hoyle only pushes the question of origin of life back in time a bit. Now, the evolutionary problem is compounded. Not only do they have to explain the origin of life on the earth, but the origin of space travelers, how they imported life here, and how they overcame the barrier of the speed of light to do it. For years, people thought there might be life on Mars. Then, when our space probes proved otherwise, scientists began to look for signs of life elsewhere. Venus and Mercury are much too hot and inhospitable, Jupiter, Saturn and the rest are much too cold. The nearest stars are many light years away. A natural explanation for UFO's is nonexistent.

The Bible speaks of Satan as the prince and power of the air. I believe that UFO's are just another one of the manifestations of Satan. It is likely that the controlling demonic principalities and powers spoken of in the Bible sometimes reveal themselves as super technological gods of the air.

Some believe that UFO's are manifestations of angels. I highly doubt that. Angels serve God and His truth, and have specific roles to play. I can't imagine Michael and Gabriel as UFO drivers.

Many New Age and occult religions base their teaching upon UFO worship. The fruit of this teaching speaks for itself. Which is more likely to be true? Take your choice: a supernatural God and devil as describe by the Bible, or super technological space aliens? I have always held a revulsion for science fiction which focuses heavily on the occult. There is little science involved in these stories, just plenty of horror, demon-like aliens, and man-glorifying technology. Now it has become a religion.

It is possible to come up with many theories and explanations for the origin of the solar system and universe. One is limited only by his imagination and intellectual capacity. We must keep in mind, however, that we are searching for truth, and examine our motivation for seeking out origins. If a person makes the assumption that God did not create the universe, naturally he will arrive at the same conclusion when he finishes his theory. Can we call the big bang theory, stellar evolution, the steady state theory and all the rest science, or is it a religion?

In contrast, creation is a simple explanation of origins by comparison. It is consistent with the laws of cause and effect, thermodynamics, and other observed physical laws.

SCRIPTURE REFERENCES

Genesis 1:6-8   Isaiah 40:22
Genesis 1:14-19   Psalm 8
Job 26:7

QUESTIONS FOR STUDY

1. List evidence that the solar system is young.

2. What is an argument against stellar evolution?

3. What is the significance of the Voyager photographs of the moons of Jupiter and Saturn?

4. What does the decay of the earth's magnetic field show concerning the age of the earth?

5. What is rate of flow in solids, and why is it significant in determining the age of lunar craters?

6. Describe creationist explanations for the paradox of distant stars.

7. What are some possible explanations for UFO's?

VIII. ANSWERING COMMON ARGUMENTS

As we deal with the theory of evolution and the way it affects scientific thinking, we need to take the evidence and put it in its proper perspective. Scientific facts do not conflict with the Bible. What we need is the skill of discernment; the ability to separate what is scientific truth, and what is philosophical speculation.

In order for evidence to qualify as fact, it must be observable, testable and repeatable. Using these criteria, evolution cannot be classified as scientific, instead it is a philosophical or religious theory.

Of course, scientific facts can be used to support a theory, but if a theory contradicts the evidence, either the theory has to be modified to fit the facts, or the theory must be thrown out altogether. This holds true for evolution, and for that matter some creationist theories.

The most important scientific skill to develop is the ability to separate assumption from fact. This is a leading cause of confusion. Scientists declare evolution as fact only because they assume it. An example: the science of genetics is observable, testable, and repeatable in the present within species. However, we cannot experimentally test its applicability from molecules to man in the past over millions of years. Therefore we cannot verify if macroevolution is true.

Let us examine some common arguments and assumptions evolutionists use and answer them in a creationist framework.

The Survival of the Fittest

One paramount argument for the theory of evolution is the idea of "survival of the fittest." Early evolutionists thought that predators have a beneficial effect toward the species they prey upon by removing the old, sick, and maimed. The selection of the weak as prey is central to the dogma of evolution.

Recent evidence instead indicates that random selection, not selection of the weak, determines which animal is eaten. Further studies show that under certain situations there is a selection against the strong and healthy, with predators passing up weak and sick animals for healthy ones. The implications of these studies against evolution are obvious.

E. Norbert Smith conducted experiments where he offered two mice to a snake, one mouse active and healthy, the other listless and sick. The snake usually selected the healthy active one first. In fact, the ill mouse often remain unnoticed in a secluded corner for hours.[1]

What does this mean? Supposedly through natural selection predators continually upgrade the breeding stock of the prey species providing the selective "force" for evolution. If the opposite is true, or if random selection is really the case, no "driving force" exists.

The Horse Series is Horsefeathers

Science textbooks often present the horse series as proof of evolution. What they actually present is a collection of assumptions. There is no proof that the fossil horses found are ancestral to one another.

In fact, evolutionists gather these fossils from various parts of the world. It is impossible to establish proof of ancestry from them. They present the horse as growing in size from the ancestral horse to the present. What proof is there that it didn't "evolve" the other way? Dr. Duane Gish points out that fossils of South American hoofed animals show a sequence in the opposite direction: from one-toed to three-toed to five-toed hooves.[2]

The Next Stage In Horse Evolution. . .?

The size of the horse is no evidence for evolution. Various size horses live today, ranging in size from the gargantuan Clydesdales to the Lilliputan horses not much bigger than a dog.

Eohippus was first described in the literature as a hyrax, not a horse. There are physical inconsistencies, such as rib count between fossil horses. *Eohippus* and modern horse had 18 pairs of ribs, *Orohippus* had 15, and *Pliohippus* had 19.[3] This is not what you would expect if evolution were true. It is more reasonable to believe that the horse is a created kind rather than evidence for evolution.

Archaeopteryx

Evolutionists have maintained that the Archaeopteryx is a link between dinosaurs and birds. Five known specimens of Archaeopteryx have been found in the fossil record.

Evolutionists said the bones were solid like reptiles, but now they know that they were hollow, like birds.[4] Like all birds, it had a wishbone. As for the teeth, there are several modern birds with teeth or toothlike projections, such as the sawbill, the pink-footed goose, the grey-lag, and the white-fronted goose to name just a few. Claw-like structures on the wings are also found on young of the hoatzin, a modern South American bird.

Creationists have no problem in fitting "Archy" into a creation model. He is simply another created bird with unique characteristics, no more strange looking, less functional, or reptile looking than any other modern bird. There is no evidence here that proves evolution.

Embryology

An early evolutionary idea is that the developmental stages of the embryo recapitulated the process of evolution. This appears in the literature and textbooks, and is a popular argument. It has since fallen into disfavor with most evolutionists because there are too many problems and inconsistencies in this theory. The idea is that the development of the embryo goes through evolutionary stages from cell to fish to amphibian to man. Although folds on the neck of the developing embryo have been interpreted as "gill slits" of a fish, it has been proven that never during the development of the embryo do they have any of the characteristics of a gill.

In spite of the evidence against it, this idea still appears in the textbooks and some teachers continue to teach it. It is another example of how certain ideas die hard when people want to believe them. Unfortunately, this argument was used to promote abortion during the Roe versus Wade decision. After all, according to this rationalization, we are not killing a human fetus, but a fish or a frog. "Because the development of the embryo recapitulates evolution, we don't really know when human life begins," so they say.

Ernest Haeckel, a contemporary of Charles Darwin, drew diagrams of dog embryos identical with human embryos evidently to provide propaganda for this theory. Though scientific literature has repeatedly published the erroneous nature of his drawings, they still appear in some biology texts today.

Peppered Moths

Another argument evolutionists often illustrate and misinterpret in science textbooks is that of the population studies of the peppered moths. There are two different species of peppered moths. The lighter variety was more abundant before the industrial revolution, and the darker variety became more abundant after factories darkened trees with smoke.

Is this evidence for evolution? No. This example only shows that two different populations can change with a change of the environment. There is no evidence here of mutation or change from one species of moth to the other. The peppered moths pose no problems for the creationist; it is simply another example of conservation within God's creation, of balance between environment and creature.

Here we should distinguish between micro-evolution and mega-evolution. Creationists do not have any problems with variation of characteristics within the species, or microevolution. The change in population of peppered moths is such an example. We contest mega-evolution, or the theory of molecules to man.

The Problem of Cain's Wife

When God created the earth, He created it perfect, to last forever. With the introduction of sin into the world, it caused the process of decay and death. Because the earth was young, there was no problem with genetic interbreeding, nor did God establish any laws against it. Only when mankind had become so polluted genetically that God provided laws against intermarriage between family members.

Adam and Eve had many more children besides Cain, Abel, and Seth in their long life. One of their daughters, Cain's sister, became his wife. Some have speculated that Cain's wife came from a pre-Adamite race, but there is nothing from scripture to suggest this.

Where Did the Water Come From, and Where Did It Go?

The great Flood of Noah was precipitated by the opening of the fountains of the deep, vast subterranean reservoirs watering the earth with artesian springs. The earth's magma heated this water, causing it to upwell and flow out onto the earth. A water vapor canopy circled the earth, filtering out harmful radiation. When the fountains of the deep broke open, massive continental upheavals occurred, causing great volcanic and tectonic activity.

The earth's crust floats on a giant sea of magma in plates. The additional weight of the fallen water vapor canopy coupled with released subterranean water would have caused the earth's crust to shift, split apart and move, creating the continents and the present ocean floor.

The Origin Of Race

Some people have made the unfortunate suggestion that the black race descended from Ham, the son of Noah whose descendants were cursed. There is absolutely nothing in the scriptures to imply this. Ham had many descendants spread throughout the world, the Phoenicians, Canaanites, Ethiopians, and Egyptians among them. There is nothing to suggest that Shem was white, Japheth was Asian, and Ham was black, as some have claimed. Even if it were the case, it is an abomination to justify racism or racial superiority based upon this idea.

The truth is, dark skin pigmentation is a dominant and beneficial feature, providing protection from the sun. Lack of that pigmentation means that the normal process to produce the pigment does not work, possibly because of mutation. In central latitudes such as Africa, India and Melanesia, absence of pigment could have become less dominant over a period of many years. The dark skinned races would have been more likely to have survived in a hot climate. Studies have shown that it would take only eight generations of inbreeding to produce any of the races.

Racism, such as that exhibited by Nazi Germany, was based upon the evolutionary idea of survival of the fittest. Hitler tried to establish that the Aryan race was "more highly evolved." Evidence is to the contrary: the white "Aryan race" is most likely the result of mutations short-circuiting melanin production. Since melanin has a protective effect, white skin lacking melanin is an unfavorable characteristic that increases risk of sunburn and skin cancer.

The Sanctity of Human Life

When God created mankind, He instructed Adam to be fruitful and multiply, and fill the earth. God set up the marriage covenant for a purpose, to bring as many Godly sons and daughters into the world as possible, eventually into eternal life. Divorce, fornication, adultery, abortion, and all other sexual sins operate contrary to God's purpose. The miracle of love, marriage, sex, conception and birth is never sinful, only man's perversion and pollution of it.

A humanistic philosophy of population control prevails in the world today, and operates contrary to the principle of God's instruction to Adam. The world suffers famine, destruction, war and disease, all which are the results of mankind not operating under God's principles. The world blames all of this on God. They buy into the lie that God is unable to take care of their needs, or did not create enough resources to sustain the population of the world. Therefore, they reason that the earth's resources have to be hoarded, and the population of the earth must be reduced. Governments introduce birth control measures, which are sometimes enforced oppressively like they have been in China, where it is against the law to have more than one child. The false doctrine of *survival of the fittest* strikes again.

We must take the pressure off those who have the wonderful gift of raising large families. God has reserved a special blessing for parents who enjoy raising children to follow Him. Child number ten from a large family should not be made to feel like he is unwanted or a threat to the existence of the world. Large families should never have to suffer such persecution. If Mrs. Franklin stopped at sixteen, Benjamin wouldn't have been born. I don't believe God condemns birth control either, but if His ultimate aim is to populate heaven with Godly children, we must choose the best means to fulfil that purpose, whether it be one, two or ten. Each of us has a special gift. God has called some to be single, giving them special ministries, others He called to have many children.

God owns the cattle on a thousand hills, and He can cause all His children to prosper. Those who abide by His principles of sowing and reaping can tap into the power of Jesus, who was able to feed the five thousand with five loaves and two fishes. The earth is not filled to its capacity. Famine and disease exist because of mismanagement of the earth's resources by man, not because of overpopulation. These problems existed even in ancient times, when resources on the earth were abundant, and before there was ever an increased population. It takes faith to believe that God is able to provide the needs of the world. But, He will do it only when man operates under the principles He has established. If we trust in Him, He will perform miracles.

Tooth, Claw, Mosquitos and Gnats

We can be certain that God created the original world perfect. But, *what* a terrible effect the fall of man had upon this perfect world! Isaiah paints a picture of the coming millennium where the lion shall eat straw like an ox, and a little child will play upon the adder's den. During that time, nothing shall hurt or destroy. That's what it must have been like before the fall.

The fall of mankind and the conditions after the flood brought upon this world a whole different order where man and animals are at odds with one another. Whether characteristics such as teeth and claws, predation, parasitism, and disease were created by God or were the results of the corruption of God's perfect creation by Satan, the Bible does not say. All we know is that creation did change drastically at the fall. Satan is an opportunist, and could have allowed mutations to cause disease and alter God's original purpose for his creatures. On the other hand, God may have altered the features of his animal kingdom to give them extra protection given the fallen state of the earth.

Mosquitos, gnats, locusts, and bugs also serve a purpose in God's creation, though it is in a fallen state. They are part of the food chain. I can't imagine mosquitos in the garden of Eden, though. Remember, before the fall, man had complete dominion over all God's creation. So mosquitos could only have become pests after man relinquished control of the world to Satan. A favorite trick of Satan is to blame this all on God. But the world fell because of Satan. It's his mess, so don't fall for that.

We must not make the claim that creationists have all the answers to every question. It seems that when we answer one question, we raise ten new ones. But, the sheer complexity of the universe is just another indication of God's power and creative ability. Creationists and evolutionists both have to take the origin of the universe on faith. It is just a matter of which is the more logical explanation of the evidence.

SCRIPTURE REFERENCES

Genesis 1:14-19
Genesis 1:20:23

QUESTIONS FOR STUDY

1. Does the existance of fossils similar to each other prove that evolution took place and one evolved from the other? Why?
2. What are some transitional steps a reptile would have to go through to become a bird?
3. What are some creationist explanations for the horse series and Archaeopteryx?
4. Is the idea that the development of the embryo recapitulates the evolutionary development still accepted by scientists? Why? What is the danger of this idea?
5. What does the observation of the pepperd moths really prove?
6. Where did Cain get his wife?
7. Where did the water for the flood come from, and where did it go?
8. What is the possible origin of the races?
9. Is population control a Christian idea? Why?
10. What is the origin of predation?
11. Can you imagine Adam and Eve naked in the garden of Eden if they didn't have dominion over the mosquito?

IX. EVIDENCE VERSUS MYTHS

There are various classifications for scientific evidence. There is "Class A" evidence: facts with little serious challenge from evolutionists. "Class B" evidence is circumstantial evidence. This can be used for supporting evidence, but is not as strong as Class A. "Class C" evidence, I classify as theological explanations for scientific problems. But, never use "Class D" evidence, which is myths posing as fact.

We must not be trapped by unsubstantiated stories posing as evidence for creation. It is an old trick of the devil to have his subordinates loudly proclaim the word of God supporting it with hogwash. That is why we must be careful to check out all stories before we repeat them, especially ones promoted by the media.

Some creation myths sound wonderful, and the temptation to repeat them is almost irresistible. It is better to stick to well established scientific facts and have a solid foundation that to risk repeating a story with no basis in fact. In this book, I have laid a foundation for creation using evidence I have tested to be true. The following is a summary.

Class A Evidence

1. The laws of thermodynamics are consistent with creation. The Bible pictures a world created perfect,

but subjected to the law of death and decay after the introduction of sin. In contrast, evolution pictures a world that gradually grows from simple to complex, from disorder to order. This is a direct contradiction to the second law of thermodynamics.

2. The laws of probability demonstrate that chance does not allow for evolution to take place.

3. Life contains left-handed amino acids, right-handed sugars and cis-lipids exclusively. If life came about by chance, it would be predicted that equal numbers of right and left-handed amino acids and sugars would form life, also more trans-lipids than cis.

4. The activity of proteins and other chemicals in the cell depends upon its weak bonding, three dimensional structure, amino acid sequence and relationships with other chemicals in the cell. Without this, life would not exist. This proves that living systems were created functional from the beginning.

5. There is a wide gap between living and non-living systems.

6. Mutations are not an answer why there are so many different varieties of living systems on the earth. Mutations are a damage in the genetic code caused by UV radiation or other factors, rendering a process ineffective. Therefore, they are harmful or useless, and not a source of new physical traits.

7. The living cell has repair mechanisms that take control when a gene is damaged. How did that repair mechanism originate, except by God's design?

8. The amounts of enzymes in the cell are regulated by processes that are dependent on the chemical structure of the enzymes produced.

9. Mutations are often reversed.

10. Chromosome number and DNA count vary widely between various species and evolutionary levels.

11. The origin of healing is a mystery, and is contrary to the way the laws of thermodynamics works. It is evidence for direct divine intervention.

12. There are many examples of sedimentary strata found with the "older" evolutionary age on top of the "younger" age.

13. Long periods of time works against the theory of evolution, since the tendency is toward disorder and decay rather than order.

14. Sedimentary rocks, which are fossil bearing rocks, cannot be "dated" directly by radiometric methods.

15. Large gaps are often found between periods in the fossil record.

16. Most of the areas studied where out-of-order strata appear show no physical evidence of movement between the strata.

17. There are many documented cases of large fossils such as trees extending through several layers of strata. This is evidence for quick burial.

18. Human artifacts and footprints are found in strata that represent evolutionary time periods far earlier than expected by the theory.

19. Unconformities, or gaps in the fossil record, are found with strata layers mixed, intertongued and shuffled.

20. Fossilization is evidence for quick burial.

21. Coal formation, petrification, and fossilization are all processes that can occur quickly under the right conditions.

22. Radiometric "dating" is dependent upon assumptions of evolution.

23. The quick-frozen mammoths found in the arctic suggests sudden catastrophe, which could be an effect of the flood.

24. The theory of evolution does not adequately explain the problems associated with massive die-outs of dinosaurs and woolly mammoths.

25. Creatures such as the Coelacanth, whose fossils were found in "ancient" strata and missing in subsequent "younger" strata, were found alive and well, unchanged in their appearance.

26. Pleochroic haloes found in the rocks indicate a sudden and abrupt origin of the earth.

27. There are many examples of animals having characteristics that cannot be explained adequately by evolution. The problems involve transitions from one environment to another, and the numbers of changes in characteristics the animal would have had to make to survive in its new environment. The examples listed in this book were:

    a. dolphins and whales
    b. the duckbill platypus
    c. the koala bear
    d. birds
    e. the woodpecker
    f. the water ouzel
    g. the arctic tern
    h. the anableps
    i. the archer fish
    j. the angler fish
    k. the Venus flytrap
    l. the frog
    m. Mixotricha Paradoxa

Class B Evidence

1. Fossils unmistakably human were discovered in strata much "older" than the alleged ape-men.

2. The dating of fossils by evolutionists is based upon where they find them in the strata. But, they date the strata using the fossils found in them. This is using an assumption for proof.

3. Many fossil "ape-men" found had superior brain capacities to modern man. The Biblical account is a better explanation for this than evolution.

4. Population statistics show that creation was recent.

5. Ecology and interdependence between organisms cause additional problems for evolutionists.

6. The origin of sexual reproduction is not adequately explained by evolution.

7. There is much evidence that Noah's Ark is still preserved on top of Mt. Ararat, and has been sighted by over 180 people in the last century.

8. The low accumulation of space dust found on the moon suggests a young age.

9. Studies of the way solids "flow" like liquids over long ages show that the age of lunar craters is young.

10. Historical records of comets breaking up show that they have a short life span. If comets and the solar system formed at the same time, it would follow that the solar system is young.

11. Volcanic activity on Jupiter's Galilean moon Io indicates youth.

12. Heavy cratering on Saturn's moons and the rings suggests catastrophe.

13. Binary stars containing two stars of different evolutionary "ages" presents a problem for the idea of stellar evolution.

14. The magnetic field of the earth is decaying at a measurable rate. Extrapolating this decay rate back, it is evidence that if the earth were more than 10,000 years old, it would have enough energy to be a star.

15. Experiments have shown that mice live longer in an environment surrounded by a high magnetic field. This may have been a factor in promoting long life before the flood.

Class C Evidence

1. The "firmament" mentioned in the first chapter of Genesis may have been a water vapor canopy that protected the earth from harmful radiation. This would generate a favorable climate for extended life spans.

2. Behemoth and Leviathan mentioned in Job chapter 40 and 41 may have been dinosaurs, which may have still been around after the flood.

3. Continental drift could have taken place on a major scale during the flood, with rapid reversals of the earth's magnetic field. Uplift and upheaval of the earth's crust would have followed. Earth expansion could have accompanied this upheaval, making room for the ocean floor and the settling of the waters of the flood.

4. Noah's ark would have been of adequate size for the task of preserving life upon the earth. It was to be 300 cubits long, 50 cubits wide, and 30 cubits high. This would have had a capacity of 1,400,000 cubit feet, equal to the capacity of 522 standard livestock railroad cars. A total of 125,000 animals the size of sheep could have carried on the Ark.

Class D Evidence--Myths To Avoid

In contrast to the above facts, we need to expose some stories that surface from time to time as false. Creationists can be guilty of spreading rumors and false information too. These are some examples coming from both sides of the issue, and the strange facts surrounding them.

1. Did Darwin repent on his death bed and renounce the theory of evolution? Many, many people have repeated this story, but unfortunately, evidence documenting this is to the contrary. Dr. Wilbert Rusch has thoroughly researched this story to its origin in an article "Darwin's Last Hours."

2. Around 1970, a story was circulated that a computer project at NASA calculating the rotation of the earth in the past and the future halted when the computer stopped on a missing day that corresponded to Joshua's long day in the Bible. Again, this story simply did not check out with the facts, and it appears that it was a fabrication. Besides, computers are not magic machines that can look backward in time, they can output only what the programmer tells them. Still, Joshua's long day does check out against the historical records of several countries around the world.

3. Many myths surround the search for Noah's ark. Various reports of the sighting of the ark have turned out to be false. Currently, a boat shaped formation in the Tendurek mountains has been touted as the ark. Investigation of this formation years ago revealed that it is a lava flow, not the ark.

We need to be very careful to circulate information only after it has been checked it out to be true. The worst kind of testimony is one that is fictitious. God does not need us to defend Him, and certainly not with a made up story. He has given man enough evidence to make a decision, and on top of that, He has given His witness within us to help us discern.

Here are some rules:

1. Check out the source. Is the source one of credibility, bearing good fruit? Do they promote themselves, or God?

2. Does the story fit the rules of common sense?

3. Does the story line up with God's word?

SCRIPTURE REFERENCES

Job 9:2-14   Proverbs 24:26
Proverbs 15:23   Proverbs 26:4-5
Proverbs 22:17-21

QUESTIONS FOR STUDY

1. How would you classify the evidence for the Shroud of Turin being the burial cloth of Jesus?

2. When would you need to use class C evidence?

3. When can you use circumstantial (class B) evidence?

4. What measures should you take to verify evidence as fact?

5. What kind of evidence should you avoid using?

6. If you have a discussion with someone who has specific questions, how do you decide what evidence to give him?

7. How important is the source of your information in relationship to the credibility of the evidence given?

X. ISSUES AND ANSWERS

I think that it is important that a Christian approach the problem of creation versus evolution very carefully, and with much prayer. Much damage has been caused by uninformed Christians who compromise, get off on tangents, or promote pet theories without giving the matter much thought. A Christian needs to deal with deep seated problems beyond the creation-evolution question.

The attitude and spirit you approach an evolutionist is important. Do not come across as moralistic or judgmental. Talk with him; do not try to win a debate. Deep down inside he does not want God to intervene directly in his affairs. Until a person has the desire to know God intimately, he will fight any idea of creation. The time when creation-science becomes useful is when a person recognizes his need for God. Answers then can be provided when questions come up and a person is genuinely searching.

One of the reasons evolutionists postulate an ancient cosmos is to escape from God, pushing him as far away in space and as far back in time as possible. Psychologically, the evolution theory gives him the excuse that God is far removed from man, so why bother knowing Him? Confronting an evolutionist with a debate will make him stiffen with resistance.

When sharing with an unbeliever the joy of knowing Christ, we can use facts supporting creation as salt to add flavor and interest in our discussion. I became sold out to Jesus

Christ when several key people shared where to find out more information about creation science. Because they helped me that way, I like talking about God's creation.

Recognizing Evolutionary Bias

There are a number of tactics and arguments used by evolutionists we must recognize and answer when they come up. One of the most common is the bandwagon approach. The argument goes like this:

"No informed scientist believes in creation anymore, that went out with the flat earth theory!"

"How can so many scientists who have done years of research be so wrong?"

"The only people who believe in creation nowadays are wild-eyed fanatics, old people, and the weak."

So the arguments go, ad nauseam. You should recognize these arguments as totally unscientific, and only an attempt to intimidate. It is a smoke screen that does not attempt to give an answer. The answer to these arguments is that majority rule does not determine truth. Just because a lot of people believe the theory of evolution does not mean that it is true.

"Broad is the way that leads to destruction, but strait is the gate and narrow is the way that leads to life, and few there be that find it."[1]

Our fallen human nature does that to us; it distorts our view of truth. We can't establish truth with a vote. God determines truth, man can choose it or reject it.

Another approach often used by evolutionists is the "barrage" approach, asking rapid-fire questions where you cannot answer them all. The only way to deal with the barrage approach is to confront it for what it is. The person using it is not searching for truth, he is simply trying to "win" an argument. That is unfortunate, for if he wins, he loses. I have a question for that kind of person: "What are you defending?"

Another form of evolutionary bias is less direct. It simply assumes evolution in everything, teaching it as fact. Evolution is respectable, creation is scorned. Scientific literature selects facts that fit the theory of evolution, and excludes those that do not. The facts I have presented in this book are not often discussed in the scientific literature. If they are, they gloss over them, dismissing them with ridicule. Sometimes I think that scientific literature undergoes a natural selection of its own, weeding out data and facts that don't fit evolution.

Keeping this in mind, we want to develop an eagle eye for scientific facts in the literature supporting creation. For example, I spotted the statement in a biochemistry textbook that simply declared, "fish have 25 times as much DNA as some mammals."[2]

Of course, since the writer is an evolutionist, he did not emphasize the impact of that statement and went on to a different subject. I highlighted it with many other observations he made and wrote it down in my notebook collection of quotes. The implication is that DNA content does not correspond with the degree of complexity of the animal or the order evolutionists expect.

Remember this when you study science: learn how to discern the difference between scientific fact and theory. A tendency many Christians have is to reject the wrong thing, ultimately embarrassing themselves. It is a skill to learn how to make this distinction and to challenge the right thing.

You can spot pseudo-science by looking for guess words. When you read a science textbook, underline in red all words like "perhaps," "maybe," "probably," and so forth. The more the textbook looks like it has the measles, the less it is science, and more it is guesswork. Real science is observable, testable, and repeatable.

Evolutionists declares that a rock sample is millions of years old, but true science can measure only the components of that rock sample, not a measurement of time. Evolutionists conclude that since Glacier National Park has rock layers in the wrong evolutionary order, an overthrust took place. But the evidence only shows that rock layers with stromatolites (algae fossils) are found on top of rock layers with dinosaur fossils. Glacier park also has exposed flows of pillow lava, which is interpreted to have been formed under water.

Another problem prevalent in science is obfuscation, which is the overuse of big words and jargon that nobody understands. Semantic confusion adds to the frustration of the person who wants to understand science. Many scientists find it hard to resist the temptation to show off, leaving everyone in their wake befuddled and amazed with their vocabulary. This is a source of intimidation for many Christians, who would rather compromise with evolution than try to surmount this challenge.

Have you ever heard the argument, "Creation is religion, but evolution is science!" This, of course, is untrue. In fact, it takes a lot more blind "faith" to believe evolution than it does to believe creation. Why? Just look at probability studies of life originating by chance. Evolutionists are hanging onto one chance in 10^{29345} that a cell came to life without God's intervention.

Many cults and anti-Christian religions in the world have accepted the theory of evolution as a doctrinal statement. For example, Social Darwinism, or the concept of survival of the fittest has a direct influence upon the philosophies of socialism, communism, fascism, laissez faire capitalism, and some forms of racism. Cults such as New Age, Rosicrucianism, Theosophy, Spiritism, and Satanism all have evolution as a doctrine. Many ancient pagan philosophies also had a theory similar to evolution as part of their doctrines.

What happens when a person assumes that evolution took

place? He then concludes that both the beginning and end of things have no meaning. Life therefore is to be lived for the moment, and for self. In contrast, Biblical Christianity as Christ taught it is concerned with the eternal soul. A Christian lives his life in unselfish service to others, giving so they also may have life. With evolution, life has no eternal worth, no ultimate meaning. With creation, life is precious, eternal, with glorious purpose. With evolution, abortion is acceptable, perhaps even virtuous. With creation, abortion is a horrible abomination, since God created that precious life for a purpose.

Who were all these millions of people who were aborted? What purpose could they have served if allowed to live? What about their eternal destinies? Evolutionists would have us believe that we evolved from animals, therefore it is acceptable to behave like animals. As a matter of fact, the way some humans behave, they are an insult to monkeys. But, get this: if we believe the Biblical creation, we are made in the image of God! It is that image that is blurred by evolution. With evolution, life has no meaning.

Therefore, if relationships don't work out, divorce is an acceptable alternative. With creation, God is involved in bringing together two people in marriage and nothing should come between them. Think of the self image of a child whose parents have divorced. If the parents think that they should have never been married in the first place, he is likely to believe that there is no purpose for his existence.

We need to realize how much evolutionary thinking influences modern philosophy, theology and lifestyles. Learning to recognize evolutionary bias is an integral part of discernment, and Christians should take the time to know the difference.

The Legal Battle for Creation in the Public Schools

Freedom of religion in America does not mean freedom **from** religion. The original intent of the constitution was to prevent the government from mandating a state religion.

However, that is exactly what is happening when evolution is being taught exclusively in the public school. Mega-evolution by its nature cannot be observable, testable or repeatable. Any theory of origins, honoring God or not, is religious in nature, not scientific. Therefore if one is taught, so should the other.

Mega-evolution should never be taught as scientific fact. There is enough evidence, even admitted by those hostile to creation, that evolution is in serious trouble. A number of noncreationists have made highly critical assessments of Darwinian evolution. Sir Fred Hoyle's book, *The Intelligent Universe* is a powerful attack on cosmic, chemical and biological evolution. Ambrose's *Nature and Origin of the Biological World* is another example of a noncreationist who is exploring the possibility of a creative force behind the origin of the universe.

There are tremendous consequences if we do not retain God in our knowledge. The origin and basis of all truth is rooted in the knowledge of God. Without some sort of moral and religious basis, how can anyone decide what is truth? Our laws are based on morals and religion. If we remove morality from our laws, we end up with bad laws.

The current climate in the public schools is to encourage many strange doctrines to be taught, especially New Age philosophies, but discussion of Christianity and creationism in particular is excluded. These same school administrators and legislators then have the audacity to claim that doing so is "unbiased" whereas Christianity is narrow-minded and biased.

Actually, there is no such thing as being unbiased. Instead, as Ken Ham says, we must choose the "bias that is the best bias to be biased with."[3] The search for truth involves reviewing the possibilities and making a choice. Open mindedness involves rethinking your decision in light of new evidence. The current situation in the public schools does not allow that new evidence to be heard. There is a lot that is at stake in this.

Should the evidence for creation gain a hearing in the schools, many scientists who have been teaching evolution dogmatically will be exposed. That is why there is tremendous pressure in the legal realm to keep it out of the schools. If the case for creation is clearly nonsense, why is it being suppressed through the courts?

What can be done, given the current anti-creation climate in the public schools? I believe that one answer is for churches to provide release time instruction or after school classes for those students who desire to know the creation alternative. One advantage of this idea is the fact that under such circumstances, the state cannot interfere with what is taught. If we wish to introduce a child to Christ, which is a natural result of this kind of instruction, there is no restriction.

Developing a Method of Study

Does it sound somewhat strange to think of the laboratory as place to worship God? I suppose it does. We do not normally think of the study of science in those terms. As a matter of fact, most people find the study of science very dry and boring, or so involved it becomes a laborious task in order to study.

What a sad commentary on our educational system! A student should be highly motivated by his teacher to explore the world God created for him, helping him to discover all he can concerning the things around him. I believe the reason the educational institutions fail in their task of motivating their students to learn is because they leave out the **purpose** that the knowledge of God brings. The knowledge of God brings life. Life creates interest!

Compare the motivation between creation and evolution. The study of creation stimulates interest because it brings glory to God. It is a world view with God in control: who created everything for our pleasure, to investigate, learn, and use in its proper manner. In contrast, an evolutionary view is one with no meaning or purpose. The theory of evolution encourages motivation by ego, and glorifies man. In contrast, creationism focuses attention on God and His purpose for our lives.

If you watch children as they discover new things about the world about them, and the delight that they find in their discoveries, that is the spirit I am trying to recapture in the study of science. God built this world for His pleasure, and for us to manage its resources effectively. Each blade of grass, each leaf and each plant is an intricate work of art just waiting for someone to discover it and praise God for it. How often we miss and refuse to acknowledge miracles right before our very eyes! They're so commonplace, they are not recognized as such!

"For although they knew God, they neither glorified him as God nor gave thanks to him, but their thinking became futile and their foolish hearts were darkened."[4]

How, then, can a student who is studying in a secular school coexist with the teaching of evolution? First of all, remember that this is no easy task. Strive for excellence! Treat all references to evolution as philosophy, much like comparative religion. Make sure that you do enough research on your own to answer each question as it comes up. All learning comes through hard work, not through spoon-feeding. All scientists are tempted to offer grandiose speculative solutions to questions they cannot answer. Because of this, it is hard for a student to tell the difference between fantasy and reality. It should be in the back of our minds to test each theory using the data accumulated to support it, looking at alternate explanations, and admitting what we don't know.

If a classroom test is given on evolution, remember that you are only learning about a philosophy, and give the answers the teacher expects. If you want to disagree with a teacher, do it in love and respect, never in a condescending and judgmental tone. Scientists would like to stereotype creationists as fanatics. Don't give them a chance. Instead, let your behavior in class be beyond reproach and let your light shine before men as an example of what it means to follow Christ.

I believe if a student is sharp and can do the double duty of investigating behind the scenes as he studies science, he will receive a valuable education. Unfortunately, most schools and most students are geared toward spoon-fed instruction. Because of this, many students rebel and receive no education at all. Of course, one solution is to enroll in a Christian school. But for those who cannot, the best option is to remember that a person learns only what he sets his mind to learn.

The next step is learning how to isolate what is important to learn from what isn't important. Often scientific studies are done simply for the mental exercise rather than any real creative purpose. When you are studying a scientific paper, try and find out the real objective of the writer. This will tell you whether or not it is worth reading in the first place. Then, read the paper to find out how he arrives at his objective, or whether he arrives at a contradiction. Make notes of important points. Use a highlighter to underline or outline paragraphs that contain worthwhile information (if, of course, you own the book). Then, when you go back and study the information for a test or a writing assignment, you can compile this information in a logical manner.

What do you do with information in a scientific paper that seems to contradict the Bible? Deal with each problem one by one. Sort out the possibilities and try to answer the question as best as you can. Some of the most enlightening times I have ever had was following up on some of the toughest questions ever posed to me. If you cannot find the answer, ask someone who has researched it more than you have, or keep reading and praying until you find the answer. Get help from someone who is better grounded in the word of God.

What do you do when an unbeliever mocks you and stumps you with a question you can't answer right away? First of all, don't expect unbelievers to act with class all the time. But react to him courteously and offer to try and research the answer for him. Then, counter with some facts supporting creation in a related area.

It is always a good idea to steer a discussion towards the basics: the plan of salvation, forgiveness, God's love and the privilege of knowing Christ personally. If you have the opportunity to share with someone about creation, don't forget to do this. A personal experience with Jesus Christ does wonders for a person's attitude toward creation-science. It is easier to believe in creation if you know the creator personally.

The Ultimate Experiment

As a youngster, I made a commitment to follow Christ as an experiment. That "experiment" is still continuing. Jesus Christ has proved faithful to his word throughout the years as I have tested and stood upon His promises. As I continue with my faith in Jesus Christ and grow in the knowledge of the Bible, I prove the scriptures by testing them. God is faithful to His promises.

The testimonies of millions of Christians throughout the centuries who have done the same is also proof of His faithfulness. Our faith does not stand in the "wisdom" of men, but in the power of God. As we stand on God's promises in the Bible, watching him intervene in our lives to rearrange situations so they turn out right, we prove God's existence over and over.

I asked Dave Conklin, a man who was delivered of homosexuality and healed of AIDS, why God had set him free. He said, "The only reason I know is that I totally repented of my lifestyle, and turned my life over to Jesus." That's the key: agreeing with Jesus about the nature of sin, and making a decision in faith to follow him totally. Many people say that they have tried Christianity, but "it didn't work." The question I have for them: "Did you truly repent?" You can't expect an experiment to work if you don't follow the formula. No man can prove or disprove the existence of God? The proof is living the Christian life standing on his promises. That is the ultimate experiment ... and it is an exciting one!

SCRIPTURE REFERENCES

Proverbs 1:5   Proverbs 26:4-5
Proverbs 9:7-12   Matthew 7:14
Proverbs 22:6   Romans 1:21

QUESTIONS FOR STUDY

1. What are some of the ways that you can recognize evolutionary Bias?

2. What are some of the logical approaches evolutionists take?

3. What should a creationist's approach be when sharing about God's creation?

4. What is an answer to the bandwagon approach?

5. What are some options available for children in public schools?

6. What should a student remember while he is developing study habits?

7. How can a person approach the Christian life as an experiment?

XI. GLOSSARY

The problem of semantics is one of the most prevalent difficulties students have to face when they study science. Dr. John Moore, in his book *How To Teach Origins (Without ACLU Interference)* has flagged a number of what he calls "cover words" that cause confusion. The following is a list of these words.

---

adaptation, adapted: These words merely refer to circumstances or conditions that exist now. Evolutionists give no explanation how these conditions came into existence. To write that an organism is adapted seems to explain something, but it doesn't tell us how fish came to live and swim in the water, or how birds came to fly in the atmosphere.

advanced: An organism is "advanced" only in the minds of the mega-evolutionist. They do not establish any criteria for what is "advanced" or "primitive." All living organisms are *advanced*.

advantage: Evolutionists say that if an organism exists, it had an advantage over other organisms that "preceded" it. That is begging the question.

ape men: Similarities between men and apes do not prove the origin of one from the other.

cave men: Men live in caves today, so why would that necessarily indicate that fossil cave men were "primitive"?

creation: Too often, this word is used by scientists to mean that something new came into existence by some natural means. The word *creation* is most accurately reserved for supernatural acts of Supreme God.

column: This word is used in geology when no physical example of the traditional geologic column exists anywhere on the surface of the earth. They use this term as if it was a reality.

complex: All organisms are complex. Concepts of "complex, advanced, or primitive" are all part of the state of mind of the theorist.

date, dating: Theorists use these terms with respect to rocks or events of the past as if some degree of accuracy in measurement existed. The time of commencement of a trip can be checked against a watch. The first cotton gin can be dated, since some records of such manmade objects are available. Since no direct means of verification is available, dates of rocks are only estimations. The age of a rock can only be estimated.

develop, developed: Should be substituted with "created by God".

evolution: When used without any prefix, this word generates confusion and ambiguity because there is no indication of the degree of change involved. Mega-evolutionists ask you to buy the whole theory of molecules to man based upon micro-evolution, which is simply changes within kinds.

historical, history: Proper use of this term involves activities of human beings; so misleading use by mega-evolutionists with respect to imagined geologic events conveys that real objects and events were involved in presumed past eras of time. Most properly all imagined narratives of geologists are *prehistorical.*

hypothesis: In careful, proper, orderly scientific practice, this term should be applied only to concepts that are testable by empirical procedures. Mega-evolutionists make indiscriminate use of this term, giving the impression that many of their ideas are in the same status as testable generalized statements formulated by empirical scientists.

index fossils: These are fossils mega-evolutionists use to "date" rock strata. However, these fossils are not always found where they are expected, and some, like the coelacanth, are living today.

measurement: Too often this word is used when the term *estimate* would be more accurate. No scientist can measure the size of the universe. No scientist can measure the age of the universe or the earth. No scientist can measure the age of a rock. Each of these instances limit scientists to *estimates.*

mechanism: This is a cover word for observable conditions with no real explanation how such conditions came into existence. Use of this word supports a mechanistic worldview centering on the idea that the cause of the conditions are known and can be determined.

mutation: Mega-evolutionists believe that *mutations* are a source of new genetic traits, when in fact they result in a loss of function in an organism, or loss of life. The natural conservation processes God has placed in life weeds out mutations.

natural, nature: These terms are grossly misused by mega-evolutionists, as if they have knowledge of or have studied natural objects and events of the past. To them, if an idea is thinkable, then the event or process is *natural.* Often the term *Nature* is capitalized, almost as if it is deified as God.

natural laws (laws of nature): These are statements of

seemingly universally applicable generalizations that are really only descriptive, and not at all prescriptive. The context in which this is used is like civil laws. Natural laws do not control or govern the universe, or any part thereof. Natural laws only describe regularities that scientists have detected in the natural environment. Natural laws indicate the existence of a Lawgiver.

natural selection: This expression really means differences in the rate of survival. The term *selection* conveys willful choice by human beings, and usually according to certain criteria (as in artificial selection). Yet, no criteria of selection exist in the natural environment. Willful choice of the type practiced by human beings in artificial selection does not occur as organisms interact with each other and the natural environment. Use of these words capitalized, as in *Natural Selection*, is a further example of anthropomorphic thinking by scientists who are committed to the naturalistic position. Such capitalization is inappropriate.

older: The term "older" is only in the minds of the mega-evolutionist, based upon fossil evidence and strata sequence. "Older" strata as dated by mega-evolutionists are sometimes found on top of "younger" strata.

overthrust: A term used to describe and explain rock strata which are in a sequence contrary to the expected evolutionary geologic order.

population: Creationists agree that populations of organisms may vary with conditions. However, this is not "evolution" since it does not explain the origin of new traits. Rather, it is a conservation mechanism.

primitive: An organism is "primitive" only in the eyes of mega-evolutionists, who do not define the criteria for "primitive" or "advanced" organisms.

reconstruction: Used by mega-evolutionists to convey that their imagined scenarios for the origin of geologic features or events or organisms have a historical basis that can be followed. This word should be associated only with reconstruction of *historical* events, where there are actual records and eyewitness accounts of previously existing constructions.

record: This term usually is associated with the activities of human beings. So when mega-evolutionists use the terms geologic *record* or fossil *record*, they improperly convey that these occurrences were actually witnessed. Mega-evolutionists can write and speak accurately only rock layers or fossil materials as they exist in the present.

related, relationship: When mega-evolutionists use these terms comparing different kinds of organisms, they convey that they can observe and reproduce lineage relationships. Actually mega-evolutionists can write or speak only of mere similarities, since relationship is discernable only by means of breeding practices to set the limit of variation.

religion: This word is often used without proper clarification of the fact that beliefs, worship practices, procedures, and conduct are included in connotation of the word.

self-reproducing: Use of "self" conveys "selfness" or "selfhood" as of human existence, or human will. No cell component can reproduce itself in isolation.

science: This word is often used as propaganda to mean anything done by scientists without clear attention to methods, procedures and practices involving specialized equipment and techniques.

sequence: When mega-evolutionists use this word when discussing the rock layers, they convey that they know the cause and effect of these rocks, when in effect they cannot. They commit the logical error of assuming that something is the cause of something else merely because the former is presumed to be earlier in time.

spontaneous: Since no scientist can avoid external intervention (of direct or indirect degree), no scientist is ever involved with *spontaneous* chemical reactions. All experiments and all observations are the result of interventions of one type or another by scientists practicing the procedures and methodologies of the profession.

theory: Used commonly for almost any idea regardless of scope or inclusiveness. It conveys status to some ideas similar to that accepted for proper scientific theory formulated according to rigorous criteria and in accordance with the limitations of scientists.

time periods: Often used by mega-evolutionists to mean "rock strata". Names given to rock strata such as *Cambrian* or *Cretaceous* convey that scientists can actually trace the age and origin of these rock strata by their fossils.

transition, transitional form: Organisms found fossilized were fully functional in their own right. *Transitional forms* do not exist.

unconformity: A rock strata missing from the expected geologic "sequence" or "column". This is an *unconformity* only in the minds of the mega-evolutionist, since it departs from his theory.

young, younger: When a mega-evolutionist describes a rock strata as being *younger* or *older* than another, he is making relative comparisons according to the positions of the rocks, and not actually "dating" them.

XII. CREATIONIST ORGANIZATIONS

Creation Research Society
P.O. Box 28473
Kansas City, MO 64118
Publication: Creation Research
Society Quarterly (CRSQ)
An in-depth scientific journal.

Creation-Science Research Center
P.O. Box 23195
San Diego, CA 92123
Publications: books, filmstrips,
videos

Institute For Creation Research
10946 Woodside Ave. N.
Santee, CA 92071
Publication: Acts & Facts:
monthly news magazine

Midwest Creation Fellowship
P.O. Box 952
Wheaton, IL 60189
Publications: Newsletter, books
tapes, seminars.

Master Books
P.O. Box 1606
El Cajon, CA 92022
(800) 999-3777 or
(619) 448-1121
Publications: books, filmstrips, videos

Bible-Science Association
P.O. Box 32457
Minneapolis, MN 55432-0457
Publication: Bible-Science
Newsletter

Creation-Science Association
For Mid-America
Route 1 Box 247B
Cleveland, MO 64734
Publication: CSA News

Mount Hope Bible Training Institute
202 S. Creyts Rd.
Lansing, MI 48917-9284
(517) 321-2780

Mount Hope Bible Training Institute is a department of Mount Hope Church and International Outreach Ministries. The Bible Training Institute offers intensive training for practical pastoral ministries. The Institute offers two courses in creation-science: a Creation Evangelism seminar, and The Revolution Against Evolution, an eight week course based upon this book.

**MORE INFORMATION
CAN BE OBTAINED BY WRITING TO:**

REVOLUTION AGAINST EVOLUTION
P.O. Box 80664
Lansing, MI   48908-0664

XIII. NOTES

INTRODUCTION

[1]I Corinthians 2:1-5.

[2]I Timothy 6:20.

[3]Romans 1:20 (Amplified).

I. ORDER FROM DISORDER?

[1]Ruth Bernstein and Stephen Bernstein. *Biology: The Study of Life.* Harcourt Brace Jovanovich, Inc. New York, NY. 1982. p. 47.

II. HISTORICAL GEOLOGY AND "FAULT FINDING"

[1]B. Willis, *Geological Society of America Bulletin*, Volume 19, pp. 305-352 (1902).

[2]Read, John G. 1975. *Fossils, Strata & Evolution.* Scientific-Technical Presentations, P.O. Box 2384, Culver City, CA 90230.

[3]Levin, Harold L. *Contemporary Physical Geology.* Second Edition. Washington University. St Louis. 1986.

[4]Alt, D.D. and Hyndman, D.W., *Rocks, Ice & Water.* Mountain Press, Missoula, MT. 1973. pp. 21-24.

[5]Slusher, H. S. "Supposed Overthrust in Franklin Mountains, El Paso, Texas" *Creation Research Society Annual* p. 59. May 1966.

[6]Burdick, Clifford L. "Geological Formations Near Loch Assynt Compared With Glarus Formation" *Creation Research Society Quarterly.* Volume 12, Number 3. December 1975.

[7]Burdick, C. L. and Slusher, H. L. "The Empire Mountains–A Thrust Fault?" *Creation Research Society Annual* p. 49. June 1969.

[8]Burdick, Clifford L. "Heart Mountain Revisited" *Creation Research Society Quarterly* Vol. 13 No. 4. March 1977. p. 207.

[9]King, Philip B., Neuman, Robert B., and Hadley, Jarvis B. *Geology of The Great Smoky Mountains National Park, Tennessee and North Carolina.* United States Government Printing Office, Washington D.C. 1968. p.13

[10]Waisgerber, Willam and Howe, George F. and Williams, Emmett L. "Mississippian and Cambrian Strata Interbedding: 200 Million Years Hiatus In Question" *Creation Research Society Quarterly.* Vol. 23 No. 4. March 1987.

[11]Woodmorappe, John. "A Diluviological Treatise on the Separation of Fossils". *Creation Research Society Quarterly.* December 1983. p. 133-185.

[12]Woodmorappe, John. "Radiometric Geochronology Reappraised". *Creation Research Society Quarterly.* September 1979. p. 102-129.

[13]Baker, Sylvia. *Bone of Contention: Is Evolution True?* Evangelical Press. P.O. Box 2453 Grand Rapids, MI 49501. 1976. p. 10.

[14]vonFange, Erich A. "Time Upside Down". *Creation Research Society Quarterly.* June 1974.

[15]"Possible Human Remains Found at Paluxy?" *Bible Science Newsletter.* 25:8. August 1987. p.1,12.

[16]Rosnau, Paul O. Auldaney, Jeremy. Howe, George F. and Waisgerber, William. "Are Human and Mammal Tracks Found Together With The Tracks of Dinosaurs in the Kayenta of Arizona? Part I: A History of Research and a Site Description." *Creation Research Society Quarterly.* Vol. 26 No. 2. September 1989. p. 41-47. "Part II: A Field Study of Quasihuman, Quasimammalian, and Dinosaur Ichnofossils Near Tuba City." *Creation Research Society Quarterly.* Vol. 26 No. 3. December 1989. p. 77-98.

[17]Baker, Sylvia. 1976. Op. Cit. p. 9.

[18]vonFange, Erich A. 1974. Op. Cit.

[19]Slusher, Harold S. *A Critique of Radiometric Dating*. ICR Technical Monograph No. 2. Institute For Creation Research. San Diego, CA. June 1973.

[20]Chittick, Donald E. Boardman, William W. Blyth, John and Olson, Robert. *The World and Time: Age and History of the Earth*. Creation Science Research Center, San Diego, CA 92123. 1971. p. 28.

[21]Genesis 1:6-8.

[22]Dillow, Jody. "The Catastrophic Deep Freeze of the Beresovka Mammoth". *Creation Research Society Quarterly*. June 1977. p. 5-12.

[23]Job 40:15-24, and Job 41.

[24]Taylor, Paul S. 1987. *The Great Dinosaur Mystery and the Bible*. Master Books, P.O. Box 1606, El Cajon, CA. 92022.

[25]vonFange, Erich. 1974. Op. Cit.

[26]Swanson, Ralph. "A (Recently) Living Plesiosaur Found?" *Creation Research Society Quarterly*. June 1978. p. 8.

[27]Connor, Steven J. "Mystery of the Radiohaloes." *Creation Research Society Quarterly* Vol. 14 No. 2. September 1977. p.101-102.

[28]Gentry, Robert V. 1973. "Radioactive Halos" *Annual Review of Nuclear Science*. 23(5541) pp. 347-362.

III. EARLY MAN

[1]Girouard, Michael. 1990. Ape-Men: *Monkey Business Falsely Called Science*. Institute For Creation Research. Back To Genesis Video Series. P.O. Box 2667, El Cajon, CA 92021.

[2]Gish, Duane T. 1985. *Evolution: The Challenge of the Fossil Record*. Creation-Life Publishers, Master Books Division, El Cajon, CA 92022. pp. 187-190.

[3]W. Herbert, *Science News*. 123:246 (1983).

[4]Moline (Illinois) Daily Dispatch, May 14, 1984.

[5]F. Ivanhoe, *Nature*. 227:577 (1984).

[6]E. Trinkaus and W. W. Howells, *Scientific American*. 241(6):118 (1979).

[7]Girouard, Michael. 1990. Op. Cit.

[8]Nash, Kim S. "The Real Face Of Mankind's Past" *Computerworld*. August 20, 1990. Page 20.

[9]W. Herbert."Lucy: The Trouble With Dating An Older Woman." *Science News*. 123:5 (1983).

[10]Girouard, Michael. 1990. Op. Cit.

IV. WHICH MODEL IS BEST?

[1]Nielson, Lewis. "Certainities, Less Than Certainities, and Evolution" *Creation Research Society Quarterly*, December 1977. pp. 180-182.

[2]Morris, Henry M. 1970. *Biblical Cosmology and Modern Science*. Presbyterian and Reformed Publishing Company, Phillipsburg, NJ. p. 65. Note: this book contains an excellent refutation of both the day-age and gap theories and is highly recommended reading.

[3]Trombley, Charles. 1979. *Released To Reign*. New Leaf Press, P.O. Box 311, Green Forest, AR 72638. p. 54.

[4]Morris, Henry M. 1974. *Scientific Creationism*. Creation-Life Publishers, San Diego, CA 92115 pp. 123-130. This book is a good overview of the recent creation theory.

[5]Morton, Glenn R. "The Flood On An Expanding Earth." *Creation Research Society Quarterly*. 19:4 March 1983. pp. 219-224.

[6]Genesis 1:16.

V. ANIMALS THAT PROVE CREATION

[1]Brown, Colin. "The Monotremes." *Creation Research Society Quarterly*. 18:4. March 1982. pp.187-189.

[2]Martin, Kelly J. and Smith, E. Norbert. "The Koala - An Evolutionist's Dilemma." *Creation Research Society Quarterly*. 18:3. December 1981. p. 139.

[3]Sunderland, Luther D. "Miraculous Design In Woodpeckers" *Creation Research Society Quarterly*. 12:4. March 1976. p. 183.

[4]Parker, Gary E. *The Strange Case of the Woodpecker.* (video) Creation-Life Publishers, San Diego, CA 92115.

[5]Keithley, Willis E. "Wading With Waterwings." *Creation Research Society Quarterly.* 19:4. March 1983. p. 203.

[6]Keithley, Willis E. "No Hope for the Phalarope." *Creation Research Society Quarterly.* 15:1. June, 1978. p. 46.

[7]Keithley, Willis E. "Hotrod Helicopter." *Creation Research Society Quarterly.* 14:1. June 1977. pp. 3-4.

[8]Shedd Aquarium, Chicago, Illinois.

[9]Ibid.

[10]Howe, George F. "The Venus Flytrap - A Cagey Plant." *Creation Research Society Quarterly.* 15:1. June, 1978. p. 39.

[11]Duffett, Gerald H. "The Adult Common Frog *Rana Temporaria* L: a Linkological Evaluation." *Creation Research Society Quarterly.* 20:4. March 1984. pp. 199-211.

[12]Michigan State University Museum

VI. PROTEINS, DNA, AND THE CELL

[1]Coppedge, James F. 1973. *Evolution: Possible or Impossible.* Zondervan, Grand Rapids, MI pp. 71-79.

[2]Coppedge, James F. 1973. Ibid. p.72.

[3]Coppedge, James F. 1973. Ibid. p. 63.

[4]Coppedge, James F. Ibid. p. 63.

[5]Heyes, Gerald B. "Stereochemical Design in Lipids" *Creation Research Society Quarterly.* 23:1. June 1986. pp. 20-26.

[6]Sharp, Douglas B. "Interdependence In Macromolecule Synthesis: Evidence For Design." *Creation Research Society Quarterly* 14:1 June 1977. p. 59.

[7]Brock, Thomas D. 1974. *Biology of Microorganisms.* Prentice-Hall, Engelwood Cliffs, NJ, p. 253-254.

[8]Poettcker, Art F. "Seventeen Problems For Evolutionists." *Creation Research Society Quarterly.* 14:2. September 1977. pp.113-123.

VII. THE STARS AND PLANETS

[1]Branley, Franklin. 1964. *Apollo and the Moon.* pub. for the American Museum-Hayden Planetarium by the Natural History press, Garden City, NJ.

[2]Asimov, Isaac. "14 Million Tons of Dust Per Year." *Science Digest,* January 1959.

[3]Morton, Glen R. Slusher, Harold S. and Mandock, Richard. "The Age of Lunar Craters." *Creation Research Society Quarterly.* 20:2. September 1983. pp.105-107.

[4]Ettari, Vincent A. "Critical Thoughts and Conjectures Concerning the Doppler Effect and the Concept of an Expanding Universe." *Creation Research Society Quarterly.* 26:3. December 1989. pp. 102-109.

[5]"Questions and Answers: If Some Stars are Millions of Light Years Away, How Can Their Light Reach Us If Creation Is Young?" *Bible Science Newsletter.* 26:8 August 1988. p. 16.

[6]Mehlin, Theodore G. 1968. *Astronomy and the Origin of the Earth.* Wm. C. Brown Publishers, Dubuque, IA. p.119.

[7]Morton, Glenn R. "Minisymposium on Variable Constants: Changing Constants and the Cosmos." *Creation Research Society Quarterly.* 27:2. September 1990. pp. 60-67.

[8]Setterfield, Barry. "Minisymposium on the Speed of Light--Part IV: The Atomic Constants in Light of Criticism." *Creation Research Society Quarterly.* 25:4. March 1989. pp. 190-197.

[9]Akridge, Garth Russell. "Jupiter's Galilean Moons." *Creation Research Society Quarterly.* 16:4. March 1980. pp. 207-208.

[10]Barnes, Thomas G. 1973. *The Decay of the Earth's Magnetic Field.* Institute For Creation Research, San Diego. CA 92115.

VIII. ANSWERING COMMON ARGUMENTS

[1]Smith, E. Norbert. "Which Animals Do Predators Really Eat?" *Creation Research Society Quarterly.* 13:2. September 1976. pp. 79-81.

[2]Gish, Duane T. 1985. *Evolution: The Challenge of the Fossil Record.* Creation-Life Publishers, Master Books Division, P.O. Box 1606, El Cajon, CA 92022. pp. 83-84.

[3]Baker, Sylvia. 1976. *Bone of Contention.* Evangelical Press. P.O. Box 2453, Grand Rapids, MI 49501. pp.8-9,13.

[4]Brown, Colin. "Another Look at the Archaeopteryx." *Creation Research Society Quarterly.* 17:2. September 1980. pp. 87, 109

X. ISSUES AND ANSWERS

[1]Matthew 7:14.

[2]Watson, James D. 1970. *Molecular Biology of the Gene.* Second Edition. W. A. Benjamin Co. New York, NY. p. 541.

[3]Ham, Ken. 1987. *The Relevance of Creation.* Institute For Creation Research Video Library of Creation Knowledge. Master Books, P.O. Box 1606, El Cajon, CA 92022.

[4]Romans 1:21.

XIV. INDEX